POSH
&
BECKS

POSH & BECKS

Andrew Morton

HarperCollins*Publishers*

HarperCollins*Publishers*

First published in Great Britain by
Michael O'Mara Books Limited in 2000
First published in Australia in 2000
by HarperCollins*Publishers* Pty Limited
ABN 36 009 913 517
A member of HarperCollins*Publishers* (Australia) Pty Limited Group
http://www.harpercollins.com.au

This edition published by arrangement with
Michael O'Mara Books Limited, London, Great Britain.
All rights reserved.

HarperCollins*Publishers*

25 Ryde Road, Pymble, Sydney, NSW 2073, Australia
31 View Road, Glenfield, Auckland 10, New Zealand
77-85 Fulham Palace Road, London W6 8JB, United Kingdom
Hazelton Lanes, 55 Avenue Road, Suite 2900, Toronto, Ontario M5R 3L2
and 1995 Markham Road, Scarborough, Ontario M1B 5M8, Canada
10 East 53rd Street, New York NY 10022, USA

A CIP record of this title is available from the National Library of Australia.

ISBN 0 7322 6920 2

Photograph Acknowledgements

Express 1 (*both*), 2 (*both*), 14 (*above*), 17, 25 (*below*); Sonja Horsman/Express 31 (*above right*); Chris Neill 3, 12 (*above*), 19 (*below left*), 22 (*right*), 23 (*above right & below right*), 25 (*above*), 32 (*all*); PA Photos 7, 30 (*above*); Retna/Soulla Petrou 10 (*above left*); Andrew Styczynski 12 (*below*); Alpha 14 (*bottom*), 21 (*both*), 23 (*above left*), 27 (*left*), 30 (*below*), 31 (*above left*); Atlantic Syndication 15; N.I. Syndication 16, 19 (*above*), 28 (*left*), 29 (*below*); National News 20 (*below*); Manchester Evening News 26 (*below*); Mike Raison 29 (*above*).

Additional research by Judy Parkinson
Designed and typeset by Martin Bristow
Printed in Australia by McPherson's Printing Group on 79gsm Bulky Paperback

7 6 5 4 3 2 1   00 01 02 03

Contents

The celebrity is a person who is known for
his well-knownness.

DANIEL BOORSTIN,
The Image (1962)

One

The New Royalty

I T was a scene of high drama and keen emotion as Victoria
Beckham, her face streaked with tears, paced anxiously
around the living room of her parents' house. Her mother
Jackie and her father Tony tried in vain to calm her as her
mood lurched between frustration, fear and anger. Fans of the
Spice Girls would never have recognized the sobbing, swearing
young woman as sultry Posh Spice, the singer with a trademark
scowl and an air of cool sophistication. In the early hours of
Saturday morning Victoria Beckham was simply a young
mother terrified and nearly hysterical about the safety of
Brooklyn, her baby boy.

She had returned to her parents' mock-Tudor home in
Hertfordshire earlier that evening in September 1999, after
spending a day in the recording studios with the other three
members of the most successful all-girl group ever. Their
slogan, 'Girl Power' was the last thing on her mind that night.
She felt frightened, alone and very, very vulnerable. Her world
had become a living nightmare from the moment her father
Tony Adams had told her about a telephone call from the
police. They had received information from several sources that
an attempt to kidnap baby Brooklyn and perhaps Victoria
herself was going to be made that weekend. It was a threat they
were taking very seriously indeed.

At first, as anyone would, Victoria couldn't believe what she
was hearing. Certainly she and her husband had received death
threats in the past. On one occasion they had been sent bullets

with David's name scratched on them. Such was their concern that for the last few weeks they had hired a private bodyguard to watch over their six-month-old son. She knew too that extra marked and unmarked police cars had patrolled near her parents' home in Goff's Oak, where she and David had been living on and off since their marriage just a few weeks before.

Somehow though the danger hadn't seemed real. Now here was a policeman telling her about the imminent threat to her son's life. For the first time she saw the flipside of celebrity, the dark side of the brightly-lit world she now inhabited. And it was scary. As she later remarked: 'It's every parent's worst nightmare, something happening to their child.'

David, who had been with his England team-mates at their training camp, had driven home the moment he'd been told of the danger to his son. He was accompanied by the recently-appointed England coach Kevin Keegan and the team physiotherapist Gary Lewin. The newly-weds were comforted by Keegan's presence. They both admire his honesty and compassion, feeling that he is more tolerant than his predecessor, Glenn Hoddle, as well as being sensitive to the emotional needs of the players who come under his wing. Unusually, Victoria, who has little time for the world of football, has nothing but praise for him. 'Kevin Keegan is such a supportive manager,' she says.

The former European Footballer of the Year tried to put the matter into perspective. He told them that during his days with Hamburg he and his family had received threats, so he understood how upset the Beckhams were feeling now. There were, however, pressing practical matters to be considered. Keegan had already named his team to face Luxembourg in a European Championship qualifying match at Wembley that afternoon. With England's finest player expected to be fit and in the starting eleven, it would create a firestorm of media interest if Beckham deliberately stood down.

None the less, the worried father was adamant that he would not take to the field while his son's life was in danger. He was not prepared to leave either Victoria or Brooklyn until he was certain they were safe. Keegan assured David that the decision to play or not was entirely his own. There were other concerns. In a few hours' time Victoria was due at the private Wellington Hospital in St John's Wood, North London, to undergo cosmetic surgery. It was the only time in her hectic schedule that the operation could be performed and it would be another year before she would again have the chance – and the necessary time to recuperate away from prying eyes.

As heads were scratched and they tried to break the impasse, it was suggested that the whole family should leave Goff's Oak and stay with the England soccer squad at Burnham Beeches, which was under round-the-clock police protection. David agreed to the plan and at three o'clock on Saturday morning he, his coach and the physio left to organize rooms for Victoria and her parents at the team headquarters. An hour later, a convoy of cars swept out of the Old School House, the Adamses family home, and made the thirty-five-minute journey to the England enclave. When they arrived, David, Victoria and baby Brooklyn were able to snatch a few hours' sleep before David went off to join to his team-mates for light training later that morning, while Victoria checked into hospital and baby Brooklyn remained in safety with Victoria's family.

It was hardly the ideal preparation for a major international match. Nor was their ordeal over. Over the next few months threats and fear of kidnap stalked their daily lives. Gruesome images with sinister messages were regularly sent to them. One particularly sick picture showed defaced newspaper photographs of Victoria and Brooklyn with bullet holes through their heads and blood pouring out. The message was chilling: 'You are going to get what's coming to you.'

Most worrying was the stalker's accurate knowledge of the

details of their lives, which added a new edge to their fear. Perhaps their every move was being watched. Certainly the police regarded the threats as genuine, putting taps on their phones and carefully monitoring their mail, testing the envelopes and postage stamps for tell-tale signs of DNA that could identify the anonymous stalker. Victoria's spokesman Alan Edwards confirmed: 'I have received a large number of calls on a regular basis from police to inform me that the gang's plan [to kidnap Brooklyn and Victoria] is still active.'

It was later revealed, according to well-placed sources, why the police were taking the threats so seriously – it seemed that similar threats had been made to Victoria's former colleague, Geri Halliwell, as well as to an unnamed member of the royal family. The unprovoked knife attack on former Beatle George Harrison at his home and the point-blank shooting of TV presenter Jill Dando earlier that year, possibly by a deranged fan, were a terrifying reminder to David and Victoria of how real the threats could be. As Victoria said often: 'I don't want to end up like Jill Dando.'

Since their elaborate wedding in July 1999 when they sat on thrones and were fêted as Britain's new royal couple, Mr and Mrs Beckham's experience has not lived up to the promises in the brochure of celebrity. The normal stresses of being newly-married, of staying with Victoria's parents, and of sleepless nights with baby Brooklyn, who was often ill in the early months, had been compounded by the added pressures of stardom.

As novelist David Lodge observes: 'Being a celebrity changes your relationship with the world. From being a private person you become also a public property, the object of envy as well as admiration, fair game for criticism, interrogation, ridicule and spite.'

It was not only the loners, the weirdos, the faceless, unknown individuals who had clawed their way into their lives, but also the multitude of faces in the crowd. At football matches David Beckham's performance is often affected by the crude sexual chants about his wife and the violent threats against Brooklyn that ring constantly in his ears. There are times when the loathing and hatred directed at the couple is almost tangible. Their appearance at the controversial boxing match in Manchester in January 2000 which featured the notorious former world heavyweight champion Mike Tyson was one such example. Arriving at the arena after dining with their friends, Mark and Jill Hughes, David Gardner, and other Manchester United players, they were led to their special VIP box overlooking the crowd. Before the main bout of the evening between Tyson and Julius Francis, the master of ceremonies introduced each of the former boxing stars who were in the audience that night.

One by one the veterans were greeted with loud and boozily raucous cheers. Finally the MC announced that no visit to Manchester would be complete without the presence of Posh and Becks, as if they were some kind of ersatz prince and princess. At the mention of their names, far from applauding or cheering, the drunken crowd erupted into an ugly chorus of booing, catcalling and chanting. Boxing fans in adjacent VIP seating simply stood and yelled obscene abuse in their faces. The hostile atmosphere continued after the fight – which lasted only a matter of seconds – and they prudently remained in their box until the crowd had largely dispersed so they could leave in peace.

While alcohol was clearly a contributing factor on this occasion, the reaction is by no means uncommon. Indeed, as is the case whenever the real royals are discussed, once the name Beckham has been evoked it takes little to light the blue touch paper and ignite strong opinions. It is a curious phenomenon, this need of the public to vilify those they themselves have set up as icons. On the face of it the Beckhams would seem to have everything going for them. They have many qualities to admire.

The couple are deeply and very publicly in love. They adore their respective families and are doing their best to live a normal life in the fierce spotlight of celebrity. David Beckham is not only one of the most talented footballers of his generation, he is also a devoted father and a caring husband who is happy to display his affection for his wife and child in public. As he and his wife have soared into the celebrity stratosphere, they have been careful to remain anchored to their roots.

Victoria, as a member of Spice Girls, gave a generation of women the slogan 'Girl Power' to define their equal, if not superior, status to men. She has demonstrated the in-your-face determination, boundless self-belief and relentless drive that are as important as talent in achieving success. It is not luck alone that has made her the wealthiest of the Spice Girls. She has a shrewd business head on her shoulders and she is well aware that since fame is a fickle master, she should make the most of her opportunities while she can.

And while both Victoria and David are seen by some as role models for a generation, neither takes themselves, or what they say, too seriously. They are only too keenly aware that the critics are always ready to pounce. They are both refreshingly candid about their virtues and failings, especially Victoria. 'I'm a moody cow,' she says, without apology, a trait that to her admirers makes her all the more endearing. As club promoter Jeremy Joseph, who staged the first club performance of Victoria's solo career, says: 'She is a strong woman, what you see is what you get. She is very open, there's no pretence about her.'

She is upfront about those she likes and dislikes, publicly referring to supermodel Naomi Campbell as a 'bitch' and voicing her criticism of TV and radio star Chris Evans for some perceived insult when she met him at the Brit Awards in March 2000. Full on and open, she hates those she thinks are two-faced. So she was scathing about football star turned TV presenter Gary Lineker when he joined with comedian Rory

McGrath in making jokes about her during the BBC TV show, *They Think It's All Over*. She observed that when she first met Lineker on a flight to the south of France he was ingratiating and complimentary, eager to win her friendship.

Victoria would acknowledge, too, that some of the more extreme aspects of their wedding and their endless photographs, which have been criticized as over the top and narcissistic, were just a bit of fun. Indeed, so keen was she to show the world that she was willing to laugh at herself that moves were made for her to appear on the spoof chat show hosted by cult figure Ali G (Sacha Baron Cohen). Both she and David are fans of impressionist Alistair McGowan, who together with Ronnie Ancona impersonated them to great effect on his BBC TV series. David told *OK!*, 'The sketch we liked best was when we're both sitting on our thrones at the dinner table and I say to Victoria: "Why are these peas still in the pod?" and Victoria says to me: "They're mangetout, Dave!" That really made us laugh.'

'What I like about her and her attitude is it's very tongue in cheek,' says Louise Nurding, number one pop star and, like Victoria, married to a famous soccer player, Liverpool's Jamie Redknapp. 'I do think that she must sit at home and laugh about it all. Good on her.'

Indeed the Beckhams have made a virtue of living more or less normal lives while being subject to extraordinary pressures. As Victoria's mother Jackie has commented: 'They do ordinary things like walk around Tesco and Marks and Spencer. Obviously they get dressed up and go out to premières, but they are amazed that anyone is interested in them.' A view enthusiastically endorsed by her daughter: 'We go home, put on our pyjamas, get an Indian takeaway and watch *Friends*,' she says.

That very normality is cause for celebration. 'Posh and Becks's appeal is that they are just like you and me,' argued showbusiness writer Dominic Mohan. 'Richer perhaps, but they still watch *EastEnders* and have beans on toast with mum.'

Yet their wealth, their background and their lifestyle immediately sets nerve endings buried deep in the national psyche jangling, namely those of class and social standing, qualities linked to status and snobbery. So they are loved and loathed and laughed at in equal measure; at once admired and held in contempt. For every fan who places flowers at the gates of their home in Alderley Edge, there are others who click on to the internet for the latest Posh and Becks joke.

While some snigger – Victoria regularly tops teenage polls of the ugliest or most unpopular stars – their presence on the front pages of newspapers or magazines has the power to produce the elusive 'Princess Diana' effect; that is, an immediate increase in circulation. As Piers Morgan, editor of the *Daily Mirror*, acknowledges: 'On a slow news day we used to lead the paper on the royals. Now we go for Queen Posh and King Dave.'

Indeed when Victoria was taken ill with viral meningitis in August 2000, her ailment was reported on TV news bulletins with the genteel reverence normally reserved for the royal family.

Their tabloid coronation came on their wedding day in July 1999, appropriately at the fairytale setting of Luttrellstown Castle in Ireland. Like a real royal wedding, souvenir mugs, tea towels and plates were produced to commemorate the occasion. The glossy magazine *OK!* enjoyed a record circulation boost when it published the exclusive pictures. Prince Edward married Sophie Rhys Jones that same month and a newspaper popularity poll asked its readers to decide who was more regal, the Beckhams or the Earl and Countess of Wessex, as Edward and his bride became. The result was only a marginal victory for Wessex over Essex. The internet proves a more democratic measure of public interest, however. There are 52,600 web sites devoted to David and 10,800 to Victoria, while Edward and Sophie between them have a mere 1,200.

It may be that future historians, who like to define a period with the name of the reigning monarch, will discuss Britain at the beginning of the third millennium as the 'new Victorian era'. 'We may even begin to gauge our times by David Beckham's haircuts or sendings off,' argues Professor Ellis Cashmore, a lecturer at the University of Staffordshire, who uses Beckham's life to illustrate a university course on the influence of sport on society. 'Nobody embodies the spirit of the times as well as David Beckham.'

The public's dismay and anger towards the House of Windsor following the death of Diana, Princess of Wales has now descended into dissatisfaction and an apathy that the celebrations for the Queen Mother's one hundredth birthday in August 2000 briefly obscured. Like a caravan of celebrity gypsies, the Beckham family have camped on a part of the sentimental terrain once occupied by Diana, Princess of Wales. They are new royalty for the common man. The Queen of Hearts has been succeeded by the Queen of Herts. So the wedding dress worn by Posh Spice was duly put on display at the Victoria and Albert Museum, an institution founded to celebrate art and design that has exhibited numerous royal outfits over the years. There were further comparisons both with the late princess and with the sale of the Duchess of Windsor's jewellery collection when Victoria Beckham's wedding tiara was put up for auction to raise funds for charity. Ravishing pictures of the couple looking like the lord and lady of the manor, which were taken by the society photographer Annie Liebovitz, evoked comparisons with court portraiture of the seventeenth century.

The inexorable rise of the House of Beckham seemed to be complete when Prince Charles spoke to the couple after a charity fund-raising pop concert, and *he* asked *them* about the health of their year-old baby, Brooklyn. It was an interesting social inversion: the question most frequently asked of Charles and Diana by members of the public had been about their children.

Indeed, Brooklyn's arrival into this world was choreographed as if it were a royal birth: the delighted father talking to photographers and reporters outside the same private hospital where Prince Andrew's daughters were born; the daily bulletin about the health of mother and child; and the departure home in a cluster of chauffeur-driven limousines, complete with bodyguards and official police outriders.

So far the toddler, who is generally rated the number two power baby in the land (Prime Minister Tony Blair's son Leo being number one) has a spoof book planned about his life, has appeared as a cartoon baby in the three-thousandth issue of *The Beano* and has found himself splashed over the pages of *OK!* magazine in a carefully orchestrated, commercial photo opportunity, organized by his mother and father. When the couple sold their wedding photos to *OK!* for a reported £1 million, sixteen pictures of baby Brooklyn were featured across two issues of the celebrity magazine.

But even though the Beckhams make a small fortune from such pictures, Victoria has objected to press intrusion in much the same way as the Prince of Wales and the Prime Minister. 'I don't want my children photographed all the time,' she insists. 'I don't want them to be in all the magazines, I want my baby to have as normal a childhood as possible.'

The reality is that in a world where the public worship at the shrine of celebrity, Victoria and David have become masters of the art of media manipulation and spin. The House of Beckham has many devotees: besides the usual waxworks in Madame Tussaud's, a twelve-inch-high statue of David Beckham has been placed at the foot of the main Buddha image in Bangkok's Pariwas Temple alongside about a hundred depictions of other minor deities. 'Football has become a religion and has millions of followers,' explained the temple's senior monk, Chan Theerapunyo. Meanwhile back in England the artist Willard Wigan, known, without irony, as the

'Michelangelo of the cocktail stick', spent many hours carving a sculpture of David, Victoria and Brooklyn so that the wooden idol could be admired by the public in an art gallery in Bath.

Indeed in an age where participation in organized religion has declined and belief in the afterlife has diminished, celebrity – the one chance we have of immortality – has become the new nirvana. As the novelist Norman Mailer noted, stars, be they home grown or from Hollywood, are the new gods. The deal between the public and the object of their devotion works both ways. 'It becomes a self-serving love affair,' says commentator Jim Shelley. 'The more we love our celebrities, the more they love themselves, then the more we love them still.'

We are prepared not only to forgive but to indulge the trespasses of celebrities in a way that would be unthinkable with mere mortals. Hence the phenomenon of 'celebrity justice' by which a star can sometimes literally get away with murder. It is frustrating for those who believe in the rule of law. Rosalind Wright of the Serious Fraud Office says: 'There is something about the quality of celebrity, the mystique about a famous person that makes it very difficult to get a conviction from a jury.'

Similar concerns were raised when David Beckham successfully appealed against a driving ban, an intriguing story, explored in full in a later chapter, that offers a revealing insight into the impact of celebrity on the media and on other institutions.

The sense of invulnerability and omniscience that fame confers is magnified in both Victoria and David Beckham by the potent chemistry produced by the bonding of the worlds of pop and sport. The Beckhams are celebrated as a famous couple, their image as individuals inseparable from one another, their duality adding a further dimension to the public's fascination. Unlike celebrated couple, actor Hugh Grant and model and actress Liz Hurley, who, as one critic unkindly noted, 'would go to the opening of an artery', the Beckhams have long since climbed the foothills of fame to reach that rarefied atmosphere in which their lifestyle has become a metaphor for life in modern Britain. The phrase 'Posh and Becks culture' is shorthand for the tempo of the times. According to one survey, the couple are among the one hundred most influential people in Britain, wedged in between the President of the European Commission and Professor Stephen Hawking, perhaps the most brilliant scientific mind since Albert Einstein.

Inevitably the notion of a Posh and Becks culture has sparked a national debate. The very phrase is seen as a contradiction in terms. 'Posh and Becks culture is really an inversion of culture,' argues psychiatrist Dr Glenn Wilson, reader in personality at the University of London. 'It is a celebration of philistinism.' In a consumer age, the Beckhams' conspicuous consumption is inevitably celebrated, envied and admired. It is little wonder that big companies beat a path to their door in pursuit of endorsement for their products. 'Their behaviour is exactly that of the average lottery winner; people like you and me, except filthy rich,' says Dr Wilson. 'The feeling is that there but for lady luck go I.'

A backlash against this vacuous lifestyle began in the Beckhams' Cheshire parish where the local vicar, the Reverend David Leaver, described his flock as the most materialistic people he had ever met. He condemned them as 'pagans', while others lamented the 'dumbing down' of Britain. 'Our culture encourages young people to worship bodies, not brains,' argued Dr Martin Stephen, an educational adviser to present and past governments. 'It is the culture of celebrity. It is not cool to be clever, it is cool to be beautiful, rich and famous.'

Of course the spectre of class lurks behind any debate about national culture, as the queen of sentimental romances, Dame Barbara Cartland made clear when she heard that the Beckhams had bought a house near hers. 'They are precisely the kind of people that one would dread having as neighbours,' said

Princess Diana's late step-grandmother. 'They have lots of money but no class and no idea how to behave themselves.' The Beckhams' reaction was equally complimentary – they had never heard of her.

In an era where traditional social boundaries are blurred and where the strict class hierarchy in Britain is gradually being eroded, the Posh and Becks culture symbolizes the changed circumstances of the nation. As Professor Ellis Cashmore argues: 'David Beckham works perfectly for the early twenty-first century, where we tend not to look for great political leaders or war heroes or pioneering medics. These are not the heroes of our times . . . I think celebrities are rather different from heroes. We used to look up to heroes, we revered them and we hung onto their every word and structured our lives around great leaders. Nowadays things are different.'

So it was entirely in keeping that David, Victoria and Brooklyn were suggested, perhaps whimsically, as possible candidates to occupy the vacant plinth in Trafalgar Square, alongside military and naval heroes like Major-General Sir Henry Havelock and General Sir Charles Napier and of course Admiral Lord Nelson himself, who strode the national stage in the days when Britain had an Empire.

While we have moved from that remote imperial stage to the cosier world of sitcoms and soaps, it has always been an accepted maxim, even in the ephemeral world of showbusiness, that less is more. The more enigmatic a celebrity, the more intrigued the public will become. Greta Garbo became a legend overnight for her statement 'I want to be left alone.' Later stars such as Marlon Brando have cultivated the same reclusive image. It was a conspiracy between star and public, each side playing its part in maintaining the illusion and mystique.

Today however, popular tastes are changing. We live in a television age where viewers watch people dissecting their most intimate relationships on confessional talk shows such as *Jerry*

Springer. Programmes like *Big Brother* or *Castaway 2000*, based on recording the behaviour of a group of people living together for twenty-four hours a day, have captured the popular imagination not just in Britain but in the rest of Europe and the USA. In this brave new world the Beckhams are well placed to stand the traditional showbiz theory on its head.

Their very ubiquity, their remorseless willingness, particularly Victoria's, to expose every part of their lives and that of their son has been the key to their success. The nation has become addicted to the daily soap opera of David, Victoria and Brooklyn. No detail is too small, no comment too trivial to generate further opinion and media generalization. Victoria goes out in a short denim skirt and the result is a two-page feature on 'Slapper Chic', discussing how Posh Spice, as the patron saint of Essex girls, is really rather common. Interestingly, Victoria insisted on buying her new home in Hertfordshire, rather than in the neighbouring county, precisely because she hates being described as an 'Essex Girl'.

Reinvention, the buzzword for every aspiring celebrity, is the key to Victoria's success. As TV presenter Ashley Rossiter notes: 'Victoria has gone from pop star to successful musician, to mother, to married woman. She never loses her edge. Victoria's made herself a fashion icon and is the current darling of fashion designers.'

It takes hard work, dedication and determination – qualities that the Beckhams have in abundance – to remain at the summit of celebrity. Like any other commercial concern, fame is a business and Victoria is a skilful entrepreneur. As celebrity watcher Sharon Crum argues: 'It's actually very easy to build celebrity, but talent is not enough. You have to create a team, like Team Madonna.'

In reality it is less a business relationship and more a throwback to the days of feudalism, when a prince would be surrounded by scheming courtiers, making strategic alliances with other powerful nobles and enjoying sycophancy and deference as of right. As one famous Hollywood screenwriter noted, when a person becomes a celebrity they no longer have friends, only business associates or serfs. Certainly Victoria's behaviour is rather more regal than she would like the world to think. When Posh Spice – who, like the Queen, does not carry money – phoned a hotel in Alderley Edge to book a room, she gave receptionist Kerry Boothby short shrift when she had the temerity to ask for the usual details: a credit card number or a contact number and address. Imperiously the voice on the end of the phone announced that she was Victoria Beckham and had no need to deal with such trivialities. 'She was fairly obnoxious to me,' recalls Kerry. 'Very, "This is Victoria Beckham".'

On another occasion she pushed her way to the front of a queue to purchase a pineapple in the Finchley, North London, branch of Tesco. Shoppers who had been patiently waiting stood back in amazement as she strode past them, paid for the item, and left the store to be whisked away to her friend Emma Bunton's house in a chauffeur-driven car. So the couple, who have their own coat of arms, live at Beckingham Palace, employ an entourage of retainers and bodyguards, carouse with other media royals like Elton John and have made highly profitable media pacts, notably with *OK!* magazine, where they are assured of cheerleading coverage.

While they are not the only stars to behave in this way, they are without a doubt the most high-profile. As social commentator Ray Connolly observed: 'It's all so ironic. In the most democratic, well-educated, well-housed and well-fed society ever to exist, in which, for the most part, the power of the princes has been extinguished, we are witnessing, and conniving in, the creation of a fairytale elite, an aristocratic caste complete with its own courtiers and castles – and PR codswallop.'

When Posh Spice mimed her first solo single in July 2000 at the Party in the Park concert in front of Prince Charles in

London, her public relations agent Caroline McAteer helpfully explained to curious journalists why a young woman who became famous as a recording artist was not singing. The 'talent' for which she was elevated in the first place was no longer regarded as necessary. Victoria Beckham has performed the most skilful trick in showbiz; she is famous not for her talent but for herself.

It is an art that irritates many. As pundit Carol Sarler remarked: 'There is to date no evidence that Posh Spice has a single skill, craft or ability worth any mention at all. Yet mention she gets and mention she loves, as she hauls her pretty butt around any place in town where there is guaranteed to be a posse of photographers.' Victoria shrugs off the carping critics, effortlessly reeling off the stunning statistics about the Spice Girls: eight number one hits, not to mention their sell-out world concert tours.

None the less, her own fame has increased since that of the Spice Girls has waned. Since her marriage, Victoria has not simply sat back and counted her good and great fortune. With the slow demise of the Spice Girls, she has vigorously cast around for new avenues for her talents, be it in music, film or television. She knows instinctively that her career will only continue by keeping her name in lights, but her craving for publicity – to be the centre of attention – goes far beyond that which is necessary to maintain her media profile. Victoria has successfully mined her personal life and that of her husband and son for nuggets of detail, no matter how bland or how intimate, to fuel the public's interest in the new royals.

When she was promoting her first solo single, she told a radio interviewer how her husband enjoyed flirting with other men and loved being a gay icon. 'He walks around the kitchen going, "I'm a gay icon, I'm a gay icon." When I say, "So am I," he just goes, "But they love me. You've got nothing on me."' Football fans, who haven't quite forgiven Beckham for his sending-off against Argentina in the 1998 World Cup, were not slow to point out that her indiscreet remarks, coupled with her previous assertions that he was 'an animal' in bed and that he enjoyed wearing her thong underwear, would only add to the crude chants he faces on the soccer pitch.

However, both Victoria's and David's behaviour is constantly contradictory. For while they suffer from that common affliction of celebrities, the 'look at me' syndrome, they consistently complain about the media intrusion into their lives. Victoria has made her views clear: 'It totally amazes me that people can print complete lies and people will believe it. You can laugh about it only so much, brush it off only so much, but at the end of the day there comes a point where you just have to say this is not on, this is just disgusting. I don't know what it's going to take to make them stop.'

Yet they appear oblivious to the fact that by selling photographs of themselves and discussing every detail of their lives, sexual or otherwise, they are the invaders of their own privacy. And when she made her own television programme, *Victoria's Secrets,* in which she interviewed assorted friends and celebrities, Posh Spice apparently saw no contradiction between attacking the 'intrusive' media and being herself a part of it.

Her husband, while more circumspect in his encounters with the media, is equally concerned about the effect of the fourth estate on his life. 'I've got to live with the fact that there's nothing I can do about any of this, but it does make you wonder,' he says in the official story of his career, released by Manchester United. 'At times, I can see why people want to pack it all in and get out the country when the hounding becomes intolerable.'

Understandably there are times when the attention does become too much, especially when those in purportedly professional business relationships turn out to be star-struck. Even one of the policemen investigating the death threats against Victoria and her family started asking her for career advice on behalf of his guitar-playing son.

Sometimes the couple have become both verbally and physically aggressive towards the photographers who shadow their every move. When paparazzi are around, Victoria's body tenses and her fists clench, ready to lash out, while David has had several physical altercations with the media. On one such occasion, at a motorway service station, the police were called. Psychiatrist Dr Glenn Wilson says of the Beckhams: 'They haven't grown into fame gracefully, and have discovered that it is a two-edged sword. They have enjoyed being a tabloid family but have also found it extremely intrusive. For their part they have fed that intrusion, while never really getting used to the idea that they are substitute royalty.'

Their confused and contradictory approach to the media is in dramatic contrast to that of a comparable couple. Beckham's England colleague and Liverpool midfielder Jamie Redknapp, not only has a famous father, West Ham manager Harry Redknapp, but also a chart-topping pop star wife, Louise Nurding. After two years with the group Eternal, Louise has forged a highly successful solo career with a number of hit singles, and was once voted 'sexiest woman in the world'. While they are not in the same league of celebrity as the Beckhams, Jamie and Louise seem able to distinguish between their personal life and their lives as stars of sport and music, constantly turning down offers for joint pictures and interviews. Louise has commented wisely that: 'It's hard enough being married and making it work, so we just don't need the added pressure of every move we make being written about. I didn't marry him for a photo opportunity, I married him because I wanted to spend my life with him.'

This is a crucial difference between the Beckhams and the Redknapps. Jamie and Louise are happy enough with a life beyond the glamour of celebrity. For David and Victoria, especially for Victoria, celebrity is their life. Indeed, far from laughing at the media attention and the whole world of celebrity, which Louise mistakenly believes to be the case with her pop rival, this is one aspect of her life that Victoria Beckham takes very seriously indeed. Her whole identity as an individual is defined by her celebrity, her life measured out, not in coffee spoons, but in column inches. Every day her moods and behaviour are defined by the way the way the public perceives her, via the distorting prism of the Press.

Throughout her life the prospect of fame has been a spur, and Victoria has demonstrated the drive, commitment and perfectionist personality needed to become successful. Her dreams of celebrity have hidden deeper psychological yearnings. As psychologist Dr Paul Flowers notes: 'There is a sense that she is powerfully propelled and has a relentless desire to be loved and cared for. In her mind, carrying this tremendous sense of neediness and unfulfillment, she thought that fame was accompanied by satisfaction and contentment. This is precisely not what it brings.'

The lure of fame can be a trap for the unwary. Many have climbed in the mountain mists of celebrity, seeking, but never finding, the summit of personal satisfaction. Victoria is by no means the first to be lost on the slopes. When film producer David Puttnam, now Lord Puttnam, won an Oscar for *Chariots of Fire*, he returned to his hotel room, threw his golden statuette on the bed and said to his wife: 'Is that it?' President Clinton was similarly crestfallen when he won his second term in the White House in 1996, disconsolately looking out of the window of the Oval Office thinking to himself: 'Now what?'

Victoria has clearly ignored the warning of Noel Gallagher, of the rock supergroup Oasis, who dismissed the notion of stardom as 'bullshit'. 'The more you believe it, the more stupid and meaningless your actual life becomes.' So when she has been abroad, the newly-returned Victoria is often to be seen with a copy of *OK!* – a magazine which could almost be called the Beckhams' house journal – checking for pictures of herself. Every day sees her flicking through the tabloids in search of any photographs or references to herself or to her husband. It seems that there is always one subject of overwhelming interest to her: Victoria Caroline Beckham.

Occasionally her lack of awareness of the world outside her own produces moments of humour. When she was in Miami recording the last Spice Girls album, she bumped into the German tennis star Boris Becker in the hotel lobby. They had had dinner in London a few weeks before but she failed to recognize him. 'It's me, Boris,' he said plaintively. When that failed to register he helpfully added: 'I play tennis.' After more blank looks he simply gave up and walked away.

She is sensitive to criticism, complaining that unflattering pictures of her have been 'doctored'. She takes a great deal of consolation from David who is always there to encourage and soothe her, as is her mother, who saves every single newspaper and magazine article about her eldest daughter. If they tell her to ignore the brickbats, that is easier said than done.

David, while supportive of his wife, is far more relaxed about his own stardom. He is circumspect in his public utterances, rarely giving lengthy interviews, and his complaints about the downside of celebrity are never as strident as Victoria's. On the contrary, he is engagingly philosophical. 'I would like to have a more normal life but I don't think that's going to happen,' he says. 'I just wanted to be a footballer and the fame came with it. I'm not complaining because I enjoy a lot of it.' Matter-of-fact and self-effacing, but with a strong streak of exhibitionism, with David what you see is not necessarily what you get. He does not give much of himself away. 'Nobody knows me apart from the people I want in my life,' he maintains, 'and I like it that way.'

He presents a blank canvas on which others can paint their fantasies; a star cast in the old-fashioned mould, silent, stylish and talented. As Professor Ellis Cashmore argues: 'He doesn't do or say anything to undermine people's notions of him. He is a kind of an everyman, there is something there for everyone.' Thus he can be at the same time a gay icon, a female heart-throb, a perfect father, a sporting hero and the fans' favourite. Victoria, who is both more complex and at the same time more vulnerable, has her own iconography: a fashion leader, a strong, striving woman, a sex symbol, an adoring wife and a concerned mother.

Yet when the applause has stilled, the chanting faded and the critics are safely tucked up in bed, the reality of stardom is rather different from the shining image. Real life finds David Beckham, the golden boy of a gilded couple, quietly sitting on his own with a specially made rubber stamp bearing his signature. For hour after hour, he stamps his inked name on to photographs of himself to send to his fans who have asked for them.

Two

Dreams
of Wealth
and Fame

S HE was a young girl dreaming of fame and footlights, he a young lad with his sights set only on football. In their wildest imaginings neither could have anticipated to what extent their childhood fantasies would be realized, or where teenage ambition, dedication and hard work would take them. Neither could they have imagined that their individual quests for stardom would lead them to each other.

'I always dreamed of being rich and famous,' Victoria has said. Certainly a love of music and dancing is in her blood. Her father Anthony Adams, a working-class North Londoner, enjoyed a short-lived career as a pop singer in the sixties with a band called The Sonics. The band covered Beatles' songs and had a stab at writing their own, but when their manager died The Sonics split up.

For Tony Adams fame was to be elusive, but not so fortune. When not performing with the band he worked as a sales representative from his home in Edmonton, North London, and with the help of his wife Jackie he began to build up a lucrative business. Jacqueline Doreen Cannon was working as an insurance clerk when she and Tony Adams first met, although she had also trained as a hairdresser. She, too, lived in North London, in a modest terraced house in West Green near to White Hart Lane, the Tottenham Hotspur football ground. The couple married in the local parish church in West Green on July 25 1970, a month after Ted Heath became prime minister following a surprise victory for the Conservatives in the General Election.

Four years afterwards, Victoria Caroline Adams was born on 17 April 1974 followed by a sister, Louise, in 1977 and a younger brother, Christian, in 1979.

In the 1980s Tony and Jackie started up Gladerealm, an electrical wholesale business, selling goods locally and exporting them to the Middle East. Tony devoted long hours to the business, which paid off handsomely – the family soon moving to the Old School House, a large, wood-beamed house in Goff's Oak, a leafy commuter village just north of the M25 in Hertfordshire. Although it is less than twenty miles from London, Goff's Oak is a rural area with unspoilt woods, commons and secluded lanes – in many respects a world away from the surroundings in which Tony and Jackie grew up. The family were also able to enjoy foreign holidays to such places as Spain and the Canary Islands.

While Victoria was disappointed when her father was late home, according to her mother, she has inherited his ambition and work ethic – as well as his love of performing. As soon as Victoria could walk Tony would dance with her around the living room, and the little girl had soon progressed to dancing and singing her way through the house. Her favourite record as a child was Stevie Wonder's 'Sir Duke', which Tony sentimentally requested DJ Ed Stewart to play on the radio as Victoria and David drove to the airport on the way to their wedding.

At the local junior school in Goff's Oak Victoria showed early promise as a stage performer, on one occasion taking the lead role in a performance of *The Pied Piper*. Former teacher Sue Bailey recalls, 'Victoria was always such a pleasant child, very pretty, not at all loud or pushy. She worked hard and came from a lovely family. She was always in school productions, very keen on drama.'

When she was eight she persuaded her parents to enrol her at the Jason Theatre School for after-school classes. School principal Joy Spriggs recalls the fact that Victoria stood out from

POSH & BECKS

her fellow pupils, winning numerous dance medals. 'The very
first time I saw Victoria dance I knew she was special,' she once
said. 'Victoria ate, slept and drank dancing.' On one occasion
Victoria, dressed in yellow top hat and tails, tap danced to 'If My
Friends Could See Me Now', the song that Shirley Maclaine
made famous in the hit musical *Sweet Charity*.

Victoria would show off her routines to her classmates and
badgered teachers so that she could always be the star of any
school show. The smell of greasepaint and the thrill of
performing on stage were a constant delight to her. She would
watch such musicals as the 1978 film *Grease* starring John Travolta
and Olivia Newton-John over and over, learning the words to the
songs and playing out the roles. She also loved the early 1980s
band The Kids From Fame, spawned from the television series of
the same name which followed the lives of talented young people
from the New York High School of Performing Arts.

One of her sister Louise's childhood memories is of her and
Victoria dancing to the song 'Making Your Mind Up' by the
1981 Eurovision Song Contest winners Bucks Fizz. At the end of
their Eurovision routine, the two boys famously tore off the
girls' long skirts to reveal shorter ones underneath and Jackie
Adams made her daughters similar skirts so that they could
mimic the routine. However, Victoria's passion for song and
dance did not entirely impress her sister. 'She used to get all the
fancy outfits and I'd get all the boring ones or have to be the
man. I wasn't happy about that,' reflects Louise.

Louise was not the only one to be a touch envious. While
Victoria had been a happy pupil at her junior school, her
teenage school years at local state school, St Mary's in
Cheshunt, were marred by bullying. Whereas as a younger child
Victoria had met with praise for her theatrical efforts, her
ambitions now provoked teasing and ridicule.

As far as her fellow pupils were concerned she was a show-off.
The fact that she worked hard and preferred to go to after-

34

school dance classes rather than hanging out with the in crowd led to her being dubbed 'Goody Two Shoes'. More seriously, she began to be threatened and abused, and often ended up in the school loos crying her eyes out and counting the minutes before she could go home. She suffered sleepless nights and used to plead with her teachers to escort her to the school gates at home time. 'Victoria had a bad time at senior school,' says Louise. 'People didn't like her because she didn't go out every night and hang around street corners, instead she used to go to a lot of singing and dancing lessons.' Victoria herself admits, 'I always used to cry when holidays ended. I hated school and never wanted to go back.'

At an age when fitting in with rather than standing out from the crowd is important, neither did it help Victoria that her parents' lifestyle was showily opulent. Aside from having the largest house in Goff's Oak, and the only one with a swimming pool, Tony Adams drove a gold Rolls-Royce. Although Goff's Oak and Cheshunt could be described as generally affluent areas, such displays of wealth did not go down well at the Cheshunt comprehensive. Victoria would plead with her father to take her to school in his delivery van instead, but she had already been marked out as different and for having airs above her station – ironically, the same things that would lead Spice Girls manager Simon Fuller to christen her Posh Spice, the name that would gain her the fame and fortune she craved.

It was, without doubt, the unhappiest period of Victoria's life – a time of intense loneliness that stripped the extroverted youngster of her confidence and left a deeply troubled teenager in its place. A later boyfriend, Stuart Bilton, recalls that Victoria was, 'a quiet person, not majorly outgoing', and says that 'she made enemies at school because her dad was rich.'

Tony and Jackie were very protective parents, but this may have exacerbated Victoria's problems. As Louise has said, 'When we were younger we weren't allowed to go out on our bikes. We weren't allowed to play on the street with the other kids. We could do anything we wanted, as long as we didn't leave the house or the garden.' Cut off from other children in the neighbourhood, the siblings had become each other's best friends, although not without the inevitable bickering and rivalry that such close proximity effects. The Adams were, essentially, interdependent – a close-knit family with few friends in the outside world. At home Victoria was loved and safe, but as she was discovering, the outside world was a tougher place and one for which she was not prepared.

Much later, when she was away from home at theatre school or on tour with the Spice Girls, Victoria would suffer from intense bouts of homesickness, crying and calling her mother from all parts of the globe: 'I miss seeing the windows all steamy when my mum has burnt the dinner and there's a chair wedging the door open so that the fire alarm doesn't go off' she says. For Victoria, home represents her deep yearning for security and safety. In the years when most young people crave independence, Victoria repeatedly longs for or flies back to the family nest. Indeed, while Victoria and David own a penthouse near Manchester and a mansion in Sawbridgeworth, Hertfordshire, the couple, along with baby Brooklyn, spend a good deal of their time at the Old School House – the only place where Victoria feels truly comfortable.

However, it must be said that Victoria's brother and sister went through school with few problems and it cannot have helped Victoria's self-esteem to see how popular Louise was with her fellow classmates, and that, while she was reduced to moping about the house, Louise had a healthy social life. So could much of the blame for her unhappiness lie with Victoria herself? Certainly it is easy to see how her self-absorption and obsession with her looks came across, even by teenage standards, as mere vanity.

Though she was attractive, Victoria had become very

insecure about and obsessed by her looks. She would spend whole weekends in her bedroom experimenting with make-up, and used to get up for school two hours early so that she could achieve a look she felt brave enough to face the world with. She would also get her mother to write notes to excuse her from physical education because she didn't want to mess up her carefully styled hair.

Matters were made worse by the fact that Victoria was plagued by teenage acne – an embarrassing problem for any teenager, but devastating to a girl planning a career in which looks and image are important. Victoria was, of course, teased about her skin, too. She recalls four girls known as 'the Mafia' who made her life hell, calling her 'Acne Face' or 'Sticky Vicky Victoria'. Neither did it help that Jackie had enrolled all three children with a modelling agency, and while Louise was chosen for numerous TV and magazine jobs, Victoria was overlooked. 'I used to work more than her [Victoria] but then I got bored of going to castings,' recalls Louise.

In spite of her troubles, deep down Victoria was still determined that one day she was going to be somebody, and although her self-confidence was severely dented, her fierce ambition remained unquenched. At sixteen, as soon as she could, she left St Mary's, with few qualifications, but with her heart set on going to stage school. She knew it was not going to be easy, but she was delighted when she gained a place at the Laine Arts Theatre School in Epsom, Surrey. It meant living away from the comfort and consolation of home in rented digs, but it was a new chance for Victoria.

It was around this time that she fell headlong in love with Mark Wood, a security consultant who lived near her parents. In her unhappy schooldays Victoria appears to have had little to do with the opposite sex, aside from the occasional crush on such teen idols as Matt Goss from the band Bros. Thus, believing herself to have met the love of her life, she agreed to get engaged before she left for the theatre school, even though she was only seventeen. In the event it was a short-lived infatuation that ended acrimoniously, Mark complaining afterwards that Victoria 'only loved herself'. Victoria did get to keep the engagement ring.

Putting bullies and broken hearts behind her, Victoria embarked on her theatre course with enthusiasm. Unfortunately, while she was hard-working and keen, the theatrical promise she had shown as a child failed to shine through at Laine Arts, and as a consequence Victoria was not picked for auditions. Nor did many of her teachers have much faith in her abilities, frequently telling her that she did not have that special something to make it in the world of entertainment. One of her teachers recalls, 'Victoria was a very nice girl. She never gave us any problem. She worked very hard'– hardly glowing praise for an aspiring star.

Even though being a starring success meant the world to Victoria, strangely she was not discouraged by such comments, and seemed to be acquiring a thicker skin. In recent years, when asked how baby Brooklyn copes with her being away from home, Victoria has been quoted as saying, 'It breaks your heart, but I think he understands. He's a tough little chap. We're all tough in our family. We have to be.'

Toughing it out is something Victoria had learned she must do. In spite of the less than encouraging reports she received at Laine Arts, she persevered and graduated, aged nineteen – only to find herself joining a huge community of performing hopefuls, turning up for auditions to find herself a new face amongst a thousand others. However, there was to be no starving in any garret for this struggling artist. Although she was forced to sign on the dole, she had the security that her parents were behind her chosen career and, perhaps more importantly, that they were also willing to help her financially. They were in no hurry for her to fly the family nest and were also happy to indulge their daughter's preference for designer clothes and accessories.

Victoria had her first real break when she answered an advert she had seen in the showbiz magazine *The Stage*. Smart, keen and pretty, she turned out to be just the girl a band called Persuasion was looking for. The other members overlooked the fact that she had no real singing experience and for the next few months she toured the country with the group.

Her love life was also looking up – thanks to her sister, who introduced Victoria to her boyfriend's best friend Stuart Bilton, a local boy who worked as a florist and part-time model. Once again Victoria jumped in feet first and, according to Stuart, 'drove him mad to go out'. A determined Victoria got her man, however, and they were together for three years. While they went out frequently Stuart remembers that what Victoria enjoyed best was relaxing at home, watching sentimental movies on television.

Although Victoria enjoyed her time with Persuasion, it was not turning out to be the career she had dreamed of. Unbeknown to the other band members she returned to scouring *The Stage* for more attractive propositions, auditioning for a part in the movie *Tank Girl*, and in the summer of 1993, answering an advertisement for 'attractive singers and dancers' to form a five-girl band. Since answering that advertisement Victoria has never looked back. Whether people considered her talented or just outrageously lucky no longer mattered – she was going places.

Only a few miles from Goff's Oak, lived Ted and Sandra Beckham, the parents of a young man who was making as much of an impact on the back pages of the newspapers as Victoria was beginning to make on the front. The young Manchester United star, with his blond hair and winning grin, was being hailed as the new George Best, a devastating combination of sex appeal and football talent.

David had a rather more humble upbringing than Victoria. His parents were also from a working-class background – his father, David Edward Alan, known as Ted, being the son of a gas fitter from the East End, his mother, Sandra, a hairdresser. Ted was a fitter's mate when he met Sandra Georgina West. As Victoria's father had dreamed of playing in a successful band, Ted, a lifelong Manchester United fan, had dreams of playing football professionally. He had trials for two amateur clubs as a teenager but never made the grade.

No doubt when Ted asked Sandra's father, Joseph West, a printer from Islington, North London, and an ardent Tottenham Hotspur supporter, for her hand in marriage, there was much joshing about team allegiances. Unlike their son's opulent wedding, Ted and Sandra exchanged vows in front of close family and friends at the St John the Baptist church in Hoxton, East London in September 1969, before going on a short honeymoon to Bognor Regis. The couple lived in a terraced house in Leytonstone, East London, Ted following in his father's footsteps to become a fully qualified gas fitter. Three years after they married, their first child Lynne was born. Then on 2 May 1975 David Robert Joseph Beckham came kicking and screaming into the world. By the time his younger sister Joanne was born in the early 1980s, David was already deft at kicking a ball around, joining his father at weekends to watch the Sunday League side Ted organized.

The family later moved to Chingford in Essex where David attended Chase Lane Junior School and later the local comprehensive, Chingford High. It was fortunate for David that his father recognized his son's talent at an early age, and spent hours practising with him, teaching him the fundamentals of touch and control, while indulgently allowing him to stay up way past his bedtime to perfect his deadball kicks and corners.

It was an early indication of David's meticulous dedication to his chosen profession – even now he is the last to leave training

– as well as of his perfectionist character. Away from the field, the unassuming youngster exhibited similar qualities of control and self-discipline; keeping his room immaculate, folding his dirty washing or carefully tracing cartoon characters from comic books.

It was obvious from an early age that this open-faced, shy young man was destined for more than Sunday football on the Hackney Marshes. Tongue-tied off the pitch, his right foot did the talking for him and by the age of eight he was the star player for Ridgeway Rovers in the Enfield District League, scoring 101 goals in three seasons.

He was part of a group of eager youngsters, which included Matthew Barham, Danny Fielder, Ritchie Sutton and Alan Crafer, who have remained friends long after many of them have hung up their boots. 'They were all soccer crazy seven-year-olds,' recalls team manager Stuart Underwood. 'They were very close knit.'

At Chingford High his friends nicknamed him the 'Little Devil', after United's club nickname, Red Devils, and while he was unlikely to make the grade academically, his skills on the football field were outstanding. He was also a promising athlete – winner of the local 1,500 metre race four years running. His games teacher at school, John Bullock, recalls 'he was always focused on football. He had blond fluffy hair, his shirt would be hanging out, his tie half undone and he almost always had a football under his arm.'

David had his first taste of international success when he was just eleven, when his team played in a competition in Holland in 1986. While the rest of the boys were overawed and excited by their foreign adventure, David, according to his childhood friends, seemed to take it in his stride. The right-winger won the game, whipping in the winning goal from one of his trademark crosses. It was an early hint not just of his raw talent but of his temperament, that combination of certainty of belief in his own

41

ability, inner calm and technical focus that is common to all top athletes.

David achieved his first breakthrough on the path to stardom courtesy of television. In 1986 he spotted an item on the children's programme *Blue Peter* about Bobby Charlton's Soccer Skills Tournament and badgered his mother to let him enter. It was thanks to his grandfather, Joseph West, who gave him the £125 fee, that the eager eleven-year-old was able to take part in the nationwide competition to uncover England's future football talent.

While he amassed the tournament's highest points total ever, easily winning the event which was completed at Old Trafford, the Essex schoolboy had his first taste of the jeers that he would have to endure throughout his professional career. United were playing Spurs later that day and a number of fans had already taken their seats in the stadium, so when it was announced that the boy from Chingford supported the home team, he was booed off the pitch by supporters of the London club. It may have been harmless fun but it was an early taste of the dark emotions and tribal allegiances of the game this fresh-faced youngster was soon to dominate.

At the time the Spurs fans would have had every right to be perplexed by his preferred choice of clubs. In November 1986 Manchester United was well and truly in the doldrums. The club was second from bottom of the First Division after fifteen matches – a dreadful run of form that resulted in the departure of the flamboyant manager Ron Atkinson and his replacement by the dour but successful Scotsman, Alex Ferguson.

By contrast Spurs, David's local club and his grandfather's team, had twice won the FA Cup during the 1980s as well as collecting European silverware in the shape of the UEFA Cup in 1984. More than that the cup-winning side contained an array of creative talent, most notably England star Glenn Hoddle, one of David's childhood heroes. In addition, they were just a bus ride away from home. But seductive, slinky and accessible as Spurs seemed, another club had stolen his heart.

Of course his father's fanaticism for the Reds played its part in the courtship – every year David was given a replica United kit for Christmas – but he was independently wooed when he saw the likes of Bryan Robson, Gordon Strachan and Norman Whiteside play for United against Spurs at White Hart Lane. As he recalled in his club biography: 'All I ever wanted to do was play football for Manchester United . . . There was never another team for me.'

As his schoolmates gradually drifted away, more interested in chasing girls than footballs, David's loyalties to the game remained constant. Former team-mate Ritchie Sutton, now a computer operator, recalls: 'When we were fifteen we started going down the pub. David didn't come because he wanted to go to the park and play football.' Nor did he want to go to discos or parties with the other lads. As David himself says: 'I gave up a lot when I was younger. It wasn't easy but I knew what I wanted to do. United was the dream.'

It was not long before talent scout Malcolm Fidgeon came knocking at the family home in Chingford. He remembers that, 'He [David] was very frail and tiny, but he could do things the other boys couldn't and I thought he wouldn't disgrace himself if he was given the opportunity of a United trial.'

There were though other suitors for David's hand. It was rumoured that West Ham and Arsenal were sniffing about and he had a trial for Spurs, although Terry Venables' – the club's then manager – courtship of the youngster was lukewarm. As far as David was concerned there was no choice in the matter – he was joining the Reds. He signed schoolboy terms on his fourteenth birthday and turned professional two years later when he was able to leave school. During the school holidays he regularly travelled to Manchester for trials or simply to hang around the training grounds, soaking up the atmosphere. 'I was in love with the place. I still am,' he says. As a new recruit he was in awe of his manager, star-struck by the senior players he now rubbed shoulders with, and utterly thrilled at the chance to play football full time. Photos of him from that time reveal a wide-eyed innocent with a shy, cheeky smile, a teenager with an engaging enthusiasm for his chosen career.

While his father was thrilled that his son had chosen Manchester United, as important to Ted and Sandra Beckham was the charming but firm figure of Alex Ferguson. While Ferguson's belief in and promotion of his youth teams was to be central to the club's success, it was his genuine interest in and concern for his young charges that was reassuring to their parents. 'It was good to know that he was in safe hands,' recalls Sandra. 'The support we've got from Alex and the club has been fantastic.' Little things about the manager – like his ability to remember names and dates, and the fact that he took the trouble to turn up when David was given a cake by United staff to celebrate not only his fourteenth birthday but signing for the club – made a lasting impression on Ted and Sandra, who now often had to shuttle up and down the motorway to be with their son.

Together with Alex Ferguson they were the triumvirate who carefully guided David's life and budding career. David has often cited, 'Everything I have done in football, I owe to my Mum and Dad.' However, he also acknowledges his debt to his manager. Throughout his illustrious career, Ferguson has set great store by his club's youth policy, nurturing and husbanding his young talent as carefully as a grower of rare orchids. The shrewd Scotsman has seen too many promising careers cut short by burnout, booze and injuries. As with his contemporaries, Ryan Giggs, Gary Neville and Paul Scholes, David was rested, substituted and kept away from the media glare until Ferguson felt he was ready. It is a policy that has paid rich dividends.

At times, though, his concern for his young charges was reminiscent of an old-style schoolmaster, a stern disciplinarian who brooked no opposition or breaking of the strict club rules. It was not unusual for him, for example, to ring the landlady to ensure her football charges were tucked up in bed before ten o'clock on the eve of a match. In many respects David, mild and well-behaved, was the model young professional. While his former school reports had regularly criticized his homework, or lack of it, at Old Trafford he willingly put in endless hours of training after the normal day was over, practising free kicks, corners and dead ball situations.

There were other qualities that marked him out: hard work, courage and a touch of arrogance, which are often the hall-marks of a successful athlete. England World Cup winner Nobby Stiles was in charge of the United youth team during this period and recalls how, as team captain, Beckham was not afraid of his responsibilities. On one occasion, despite having missed a penalty in open play during an important semi-final game in the Milk Cup Youth Tournament, he was the first to volunteer when it came to a penalty shoot-out. Stiles recalls 'He was determined to stand up and be counted and he has continued to show that great character. He has taken a tremendous amount of stick over the last few years, but the great thing about David is that he doesn't let it get to him.'

At the age of nineteen, David had a short spell on loan to Preston North End, a Third Division side at the time. There, he briefly experienced the world of hard knocks away from the cosy confines of Old Trafford. While he returned to make his first team debut for the Reds in the Premier League against Leeds United in April 1995, his temporary relegation to the lower reaches of the football kingdom made him all the more determined to succeed.

Away from the ground he was equally dedicated. Rather than nights on the town, he regularly stayed in at his digs, reserving his energy for the next day on the pitch. He was happy to relax watching the TV, reading books by writers such as Stephen King, or listening to his preferred rap music. When he did go out it was with his fellow apprentices in the youth squad, notably Gary and Phil Neville, Ryan Giggs, Ben Thornley and Dave Gardner. Even in this ambitious and highly talented group of friends, David stood out as being, at times, rather prissily conscientious. After a night out at the cinema rounded off with a pizza, David was ribbed by his friends when he ordered milk rather than beer. Worried that he was too scrawny for the big time, he thought this would build up his body.

In a profession where discipline and team spirit are paramount, Ferguson takes a dim view of individualism, and the normal teenage opportunities to rebel or to stand out from the crowd were strictly limited. However, there had to be some outlets for the youngsters to show off their success and the fruits of hard labour. In David's case he developed a passion for fast cars which he personalized, and also a taste for playing the dandy in designer clothes.

As well as devoting much time to his image and appearance, David also started to put more effort into his social life. Whereas, when he was younger, he had had no time for the opposite sex, he now started to date girls whom he met through the Manchester United circle. He briefly dated blonde air stewardess Lisa Rys-Halska, and his short romance with Julie Killelea, a part-time model and daughter of wealthy United supporter Robert Killelea, was talked of in the press as a 'real love match'.

David had other relationships but his girlfriends complained of a lack of commitment, receiving the impression that he would rather be making passes on the soccer pitch than in the bedroom. Model Leoni Marzell dated him on and off for a year, but admitted that he only came alive when talking about soccer to her father at their home in Waltham Abbey. When he made a date with former Miss UK Anna Bartley, after meeting her at a Manchester United supporters' club function, his social skills left her distinctly underwhelmed. 'He took me to a restaurant but said almost nothing,' the former psychology student was reported as saying. 'He wasn't great at conversation.' Others were more charitable. 'He was the perfect gentleman,' remembers Belinda Gibson, the sister of former Tottenham and Manchester United player Terry Gibson, who dated him for two months.

Football can be an incestuous and claustrophobic world with little opportunity to meet people outside its environs. Soon after David and Julie Killelea split up, Julie started dating Phil Neville, to whom she is now married, while Lisa ended up dating Ryan Giggs, on one occasion losing her driving licence while taking him home after a late night drinking session in a Manchester nightclub. In spite of the easy access to friends and family of other players and to the beautiful and glamorous hangers on who adorned the Manchester United circle, David had yet to meet the woman for him.

While his love life was not running smoothly, David's career was in top gear. By 1996 he had already won the double with his club and had been picked to play for England by his childhood hero, now team coach, Glenn Hoddle. He was so thrilled to be elevated to such illustrious company that the young man took along his autograph book to collect signatures. And it was while he was with the England team that the missing piece in an otherwise seemingly perfect young life fell within his grasp.

He was relaxing in a hotel in Tblisi, Georgia, in November 1996 with his room-mate and best friend Gary Neville when he noticed a video of the Spice Girls' second number one hit, 'Say You'll Be There', playing on the TV. He recalls: 'I pointed at the screen and told Gary, "That's the girl for me and I am going to get her." It was her eyes, her face. She's my idea of perfection. I was sure just from seeing her on that video. That she was the one I wanted, and I knew that if she wanted me we would be together forever.'

In fact the pop video, complete with fast cars, laser guns and special effects, portrayed Victoria as a screen dominatrix, dressed from head to foot in a black PVC cat suit, sporting a dark wig. She was only glimpsed in very short bursts as she played the part of fantasy screen babe, Midnight Miss Suki. While David fell for the challenge of the dominant, unattainable woman, when Victoria was making the film, romance was the last thing on her mind. She was forced to perch on the back of a car in the searing 112 degrees heat of the Mojave Desert for an hour while the director got the shot he wanted.

Coincidentally, a few days after he returned from the match, which England won, Victoria appeared in the *Sun* newspaper wearing a Manchester United strip, which she had donned to please manager Simon Fuller – a keen United fan. As it happened Victoria's romance with Stuart Bilton was fizzling out. Her whirlwind lifestyle, rubbing shoulders with the likes of Prince Charles and former South African President Nelson Mandela, was something that Stuart didn't feel he could relate to. She was away touring for months at a time and inevitably their relationship foundered.

Victoria, too, remembers that she was attracted to David some time before the couple met in person, having favoured his photograph over those of other footballers in a soccer magazine interview she was shown. 'I fancied David long before I met him,' she recalls. 'I had no idea who he was but I just remember thinking he was gorgeous. He just seemed ideal – sensitive, sexy, good-looking, funny, confident but not arrogant – all the qualities I look for in a man.'

Interestingly David Beckham may not have been the only one she had eyes for. Apparently when the Spice Girls were just struggling wannabes, she idolized his team-mate Ryan Giggs.

While Stuart Bilton was recovering in hospital following a

serious skiing accident during a holiday with Victoria's father and other friends, Victoria found herself with an opportunity to get a closer look at the sexy footballer whose looks had caught her eye. She went to watch David play at Chelsea, and after the game went to the players' lounge. The couple waved to one another across the crowded room, but both were too shy to make closer contact.

It was an intensely frustrating moment for David: 'It was the moment I'd waited for and I blew it,' he said. Victoria's appetite was whetted, however. The relationship with Stuart was over and when on 15 March 1997 she was offered the chance to go with keen football fan Melanie Chisholm (a Liverpool supporter) to see David in action against Sheffield Wednesday, she jumped at it. Victoria may have set her sights on the midfielder, but according to one source she forgot to take her glasses along to the match and had no idea which of the men in action was David. This time Victoria was not going to let her quarry escape, however, walking purposefully over to him in the player's bar and complimenting him on his play. 'We really did get on from that first moment,' she recalls. 'I could see he was shy which I thought, for someone so well known, was really attractive.'

David was equally relieved. 'As soon as she smiled I knew everything was going to be OK and we had a great night,' he recalls. 'We went out together and arranged to meet again a few days later.

As with his previous girlfriends, David was a rather bashful suitor. It wasn't until the fourth date that they even shared a kiss. But their courtship was off to a sure if slow start. It did not take them long to realize that their lives had much in common. Importantly they shared and understood the pleasures and pressures of being at the height of a career they loved, but they also both came from close-knit and loving families whose values were important to them. Neither had looked for or had the chance to explore a wild adolescence and both were highly dedicated perfectionists prepared to give as well as to give up whatever it took to get to where they wanted to be.

What they wanted from each other was trust and understanding, but also the reassurance of mutual admiration. In a sense that they were each other's trophies – slightly disbelieving that they had won each other, but immensely pleased and flattered to have done so. It is a common phenomenon in the world of celebrity. As psychiatrist Dr Glenn Wilson explains, while David and Victoria are deeply in love, their status gives them the opportunity for mutual worship, transferring their fantasies on to one another. They not only bolster each other's egos, but in mirroring each other fulfil their narcissistic tendencies.

Victoria has admitted that much of her initial attraction to David was because she saw in him someone like her – well known and well off. 'Everyone used to ask if my initial attraction to David was the fact that he was famous. I always said it wasn't but actually that was a lie. If someone is really talented, as a footballer or an artist or an academic, the point isn't that they are famous, but they are talented and dedicated. The fact that we are in the same position makes us equal and it is quite ironic the way our careers run parallel. When we first met I was on my first album and he was playing in his first proper first team season . . . We are equally famous and attract equal attention.'

Equally famous, but there were crucial differences. To David to play football for Manchester United was the horizon of his ambitions. As far as he was concerned, celebrity took second place. 'I just wanted to be a footballer and fame came with it,' he admitted in the club magazine. By contrast, Victoria's supreme ambition, the thought she has had since childhood, is to be famous and admired. For her celebrity is an achievement in itself, her work with the Spice Girls a vehicle to allow her to fulfil her dream. Similarly, while it can be said that both of them have been lucky, and that both owe their success to the careful nurturing of others – in David's case Alex Ferguson and the Manchester United machine, in Victoria's Simon Fuller – success has been much more gradual for David. His talent has been unquestioned since he was a small boy and increasingly recognized and praised as he matured into an undoubtedly first-class player. In contrast Victoria's success has been achieved quickly, and in spite of rather than because of any real talent she can demonstrate.

As one commentator noted: 'Home Counties children David Beckham and Victoria Adams could easily have met in a West End nightclub, fallen in love, married and lived happily ever after like thousands of other anonymous couples. Two things prevented it – his prodigious football talent and her good fortune in being plucked from obscurity for the Spice Girls. Beckham, as arguably the most talented English footballer of his era, would no doubt be famous whoever his wife was.'

Yet, in the early months of their relationship, the couple's overriding concern was for each other. It was noted that they acted like a couple of teenagers head over heels in love for the first time. Indeed, there was almost a childlike innocence about their relationship. While they tried to the keep the romance a secret from the world, they also grinned at the eager press cameramen, who had not been slow to wake up to the fact that the combination of a world-class footballer and a world-famous pop star was a media gift from heaven. The paparazzi were on their tail – snapping away at Victoria leaving David's house or during the couple's romantic weekend away in St Tropez. 'We seemed to have every photographer in the world following us which was really difficult,' says Victoria.

Whenever they could be together the couple were soon inseparable, preferring to stay in and cuddle on the sofa, watching television and eating takeaway curry than be out having nights on the town. When, more often than not, they were forced to be apart, they spent hours on the telephone, discussing the minutiae of their lives. If, for example, David was in a restaurant he would ring up Victoria, wherever she was in the world, to talk about what he should have for a starter. Then he would call again to debate the main course. It is even said that when they were apart, Victoria would go to bed wearing one of David's England shirts. They also began to exchange expensive presents and began their ongoing preference for his and hers items. They were spotted wearing matching designer Rolex watches, and while Victoria claims it is just a laugh that they sometimes dress identically, it is also a public statement that they belong together, as well as being guaranteed to generate publicity.

While Victoria's fellow Spice Girls seemed to approve of David, making time for the couple to be alone, and happy for him to join Victoria on tour or backstage, David's United colleagues were quick to give him a good ribbing about the love match. Not slow to see the changes in David his friends made fun of him. Ryan Giggs especially liked to ring up David's mobile phone pretending to be Victoria and cooing 'I love you' before bursting into laughter. Meanwhile Gary Neville observed, 'He was coming to training every day and he was like a little schoolboy.' Yet his team-mates cannot always afford to be so good-humoured about the relationship. Victoria has explained that when David knows she will be at a game he always meets her before the start of play, becoming agitated if she is late and unable to relax until she is safely seated. For this reason, none of David's team mates can relax either.

While the United players teased him, Alex Ferguson took a stronger stance – not impressed to find that if his formerly model player was not on the telephone to his new love, he was chartering planes to see her – especially to Ireland where Victoria stayed for a year as a tax exile. David flew to Barcelona to watch a Spice Girls concert and appeared backstage at another show at Wembley arena.

During the courtship there were glimpses, too, of the more normal anxieties and fears that assail a young, good-looking couple who are forced, by dint of their careers, to stay apart for long periods. While admitting that she trusted her lover implicitly, there were the inevitable doubts and worries, Victoria admitting that she phoned David late at night to check that he was home safely. Left unsaid was her fear that he could be with another woman. 'Are they going out? What are they doing? . . . it's always in the back of your mind when you're so far away,' she confessed.

Yet their love for each other deepened and proved more than capable of withstanding the problems of distance, career commitments, and the considerable distractions of being played out in the public eye. By June of that year there had already been rumours circulating that the couple were about to announce their engagement and Victoria was photographed coming out of a bridal shop. Speculation increased when Victoria appeared in the papers at Christmas wearing a £13,000 diamond-studded cross – her Christmas present from David. Spokespeople for the Spice Girls laughed off the notion of a 'Posh' wedding, with Victoria herself telling *USA Today*, 'I don't see any ring do you?'

However, behind the scenes, Tony Adams found himself being paid a visit by David to ask for his eldest daughter's hand in marriage – the most nerve-wracking moment in David's life. He need not have worried. David had proved to be a big hit with the Adams family, especially with Jackie Adams, whom he had won over not just because of the self-evident fact that he adored her daughter, but because he was down to earth – happy to offer to wash up after a meal with the family. Having been given permission, David in the true tradition went down on one knee to ask Victoria to be his wife. She did not hesitate in saying yes but then produced her own ring. 'Don't forget girl power – will you marry me?' she reportedly asked.

In January 1998, a mere ten months after they first met, the couple announced their engagement, appearing before the media at a photo call somewhat reminiscent of royal occasions. Victoria had flown in from Los Angeles where she had been working on *Spiceworld: The Movie,* and linked up with David at the elegant Rookery Hall Hotel in Nantwich, Cheshire. The couple actually overslept and there was hardly a moment to prepare themselves for the inevitable photographs – the press conference having been set for 11 a.m. In the event, they were forced to keep everyone waiting. As they proudly showed off their rings – hers a diamond solitaire costing over £40,000, his a diamond and gold band she had chosen with the help of her parents at a Hollywood jeweller – Victoria told the world's media it was just what she wanted, adding somewhat coyly that it had all been 'a big surprise'. Meanwhile David told reporters: 'I could not be happier right now. I have my dream woman.'

Though some pointed out cynically that the announcement was perfectly timed to coincide with the release of *Spiceworld* in the US, and although even the Posh & Becks romance could not compete commercially with that portrayed by Kate Winslet and Leonardo DiCaprio in *Titanic,* two, it would seem, were set to become one.

Three

The Famous Five

A T the Spice Girls offices in central London, photographs of all the girls adorn the walls including a life-size portrait of Geri Halliwell. There is one difference; her picture is upside down, her legs spread out in a 'V' sign. No doubt it is a telling indication of the sense of betrayal and bitterness felt by the others when she walked out on the band on the eve of their American tour.

Indeed at Brooklyn's first birthday party, it did not escape notice that when the DJ inadvertently played a song by the ginger-haired star it was quickly taken off. In public Victoria, who admits that she is a real chatterbox, is reduced to silence by the mention of Geri's name. It is as though she is trying to contain herself; as if giving vent to her feelings would expose the depth of the hurt and anger she felt at her abrupt departure from the pop group that became at once a musical and cultural phenomenon.

It wasn't always like this. Before the Spice Girls changed their lives for ever, Geri and Victoria were just two more wannabes with dreams of the big time, every week scouring the showbiz magazine *The Stage* in the hope of spotting that special job advert that would be their passport to stardom. They met in the foyer of the Trocadero cinema in the West End in the spring of 1994, sharing a stolen bag of popcorn before they auditioned for a possible part in the movie *Tank Girl*.

The result was another rejection, another blow to the ego – and another week waiting for the arrival of *The Stage* to see if opportunity would finally knock on their doors. A few weeks later each noticed independently an ad in *The Stage* for an all-girl band. Those who were 'streetwise, ambitious, determined and outgoing' were asked to apply. Victoria needed no second invitation. She and 400 other hopefuls were each permitted a 30-second audition, her song and dance routine seeing her through to the shortlist. The girls were selected by the father and son team, Chris and Bob Herbert who, backed by financier Chic Murphy, had the idea of creating an all-girl group to match the success of boy bands like Take That, East 17 and New Kids on the Block. It was a purely commercial pop exercise, dreamed up by enterprising businessmen. Girl Power was the last thing on their minds.

After a second audition in April 1994, Victoria, Geri, Mel Brown, Melanie Chisholm and student Michelle Stephenson were chosen for the group. They had to give up all other work, holidays, and other auditions to concentrate on turning themselves into a group, provisionally called Touch. For a time they shared rooms at a bed and breakfast in Surrey. Victoria, who arrived with two huge suitcases filled with clothes, roomed with Geri. Glamorous it was not. The girls, now on the dole, rehearsed in Trinity Studios in Woking, Surrey, a rundown dance hall run by a music charity.

Their first musical efforts were as woeful as the surroundings. Pianist Ian Lee recalls: 'They sounded absolutely awful. Geri had problems singing in tune and none of them could move together. After a few days you could see something gelling, but it was not an overnight miracle.' In fact it took two years of hard work before they became 'an overnight success'. 'They worked like slaves to get things right,' he recalls. While it helped that Victoria, Mel C and Mel B had dance training, the girls were regularly working from early morning until late into the evening, endlessly practising their routines and their singing. Occasionally they would put on an impromptu show for visiting council dignitaries. Ian recalls: 'They loved the opportunity to show off. They were a laugh and we all got on really well.'

The girls moved to a three-bedroomed semi-detached Wimpey house in Maidenhead, Berkshire, Victoria now sharing with Michelle who was never as committed as the others. She eventually left to be replaced by blonde Emma Bunton, then just eighteen. As the youngest in the group, she was, like her new roommate, often homesick; Victoria ferried her regularly to her mother's home in North London. 'I like going out with Victoria because she goes to posh places,' said Emma. 'When you catch her on a funny day, you won't stop laughing. She's got a really dry sense of humour.'

She needed it. Communal life in the house in Maidenhead was something of a shock after leafy Goff's Oak; the morning rush for the bathroom, the washing-up rota and of course the queue to use the house phone. Mealtimes were as haphazard as their different, rather faddy diets. Geri, who has admitted suffering from the eating disorder, anorexia nervosa, had ongoing problems while the other girls had their own quirks. Mel C loved mashed potatoes and tomato ketchup, Emma, the youngest, dieted on baby food, while Victoria existed on a diet of cheese and crackers with the occasional bagel with honey. Only Mel B made herself proper meals.

Of course there were rows and personality clashes, but when the girls look back on those days they remember only the good times. As Victoria has recalled: 'We know each other so well, and we've all seen each other happy, sad, crying, whatever, that we're totally comfortable with each other.' While the girls got on well, Victoria's personality got rather submerged in the group dynamics. Victoria was a little intimidated by the experience of Geri, the oldest girl in the group and Mel B's raucous, argumentative nature, and she was creatively over-shadowed by Mel Chisholm who was acknowledged as the best singer in the band. Certainly Geri and Melanie Brown were the accepted leaders of the group, fighting like cat and dog over everything from choreography to singing style. 'Geri would stand there with her arms by her sides and her fists clenched as Mel would have a go at her for singing out of tune,' recalls Ian Lee. 'Mel Chisholm would always act the peacemaker and the other girls would just watch in stunned silence.'

Victoria had other talents, as Geri recalls in her auto-biography: 'I had a wild imagination and chaotic creativity, but I didn't have the skills or training to channel them properly. Mel C had a great voice, but was camera-shy and introverted; she hated even talking on the telephone. Mel B had amazing energy, but was a loose cannon who never quite knew what she was aiming at or why it was important to her. Victoria perhaps wasn't the most creative, but she had something far more valuable and important to the group – a sensible and normal outlook on life. She could keep our feet on the ground when our ambitions outstripped our abilities.'

It was Victoria who paid closest attention to the contracts which their musical mentors asked them to sign in February 1995 when they considered their act was good enough to launch on to an unsuspecting world. After consulting with her businessman father, Victoria convinced the others that the percentage their erstwhile managers wanted to take was too high. One evening, while the girls were sitting chatting in their house in Maidenhead, Victoria put forward the suggestion that they should leave Bob and Chris. It was an idea seized on by the others, particularly Geri. The girls were no longer raw recruits but a well-trained, professional outfit who knew they had something special to offer. They were well rehearsed, their strengths were amplified, and their weaknesses downplayed. In short they had what it takes. As Ian Lee recalls: 'You could see they were going to make it.'

It was not going to be easy. After a major bust-up with the Herberts in April 1995, the girls were left homeless, hawking their talents around Tin Pan Alley. They travelled to Sheffield to team up with songwriter Eliot Kennedy, who had penned hits for Take That, while in London two other songwriters, Matt Rowe and Richard Stannard helped them write the song that was to make their name, 'Wannabe'.

They realized that they needed a manager who was as ambitious as they were. They found him in the shape of Simon Fuller, who already had Annie Lennox and disco diva Cathy Dennis on his books. At their first meeting the girls, then still on the dole, talked about their hopes and dreams. They wanted movies, merchandising, TV specials, the lot. 'We want to be as famous as Persil Automatic,' quipped Victoria. For his part he told the girls that they would make it big, with or without him, but if they followed his guidance he would take them in the direction they wanted to go.

They took him at his word and agreed to allow him to act for them. First Fuller had to sort out the mess the girls had left behind, settling their contractual dispute with the Herberts and then setting about finding a record deal for the band. While some have seen this story as a triumph of artist over management, others, more cynically and perhaps realistically, describe the changeover as treating the girls rather like professional footballers, selling them from one management to another for a sum neither side would disclose.

No matter, over the next few months and years, Victoria quietly learned at the feet of the master, her business brain soaking up the way their new smooth-talking Svengali operated. She realized almost instinctively that success in showbiz was not just about talent but more importantly, hard work, enterprise and control. The control of image mattered most; planning, placement, public relations and promotion were all vital ingredients.

Understandably she lost her famous self-control when the girls celebrated signing their first recording contract with

Virgin Records in July 1995. At a champagne reception on the rooftop of Virgin headquarters, they signed a rumoured £2 million deal. On the way home Victoria, high on drink and the exhilaration of the day, threw her knickers out of the taxi. That same effervescent spirit – and acute sense of publicity – was on show a few months later when the girls performed 'Wannabe' around the bronze statue of Red Rum at Kempton racecourse, much to the annoyance of race officials. It was their ebullient high spirits and comradeship, later defined as Girl Power, that impressed those who were working with them on their first single and album. Producer Matt Rowe recalls: 'Everything was there, right from the beginning, the attitude, the philosophy, the Girl Power thing. They had all the ideas for the songs, and we'd sort of piece them together like a jigsaw puzzle.'

The jigsaw puzzle started coming together in early 1996 when a video of their first single was shown on cable TV and proved such a success that it was repeated 70 times in a week. After the video came the release of the single in Japan to test the commercial waters. The bean-counters need not have worried; 'Wannabe' sold more than any of the Beatles' records. In July 1996 'Wannabe' was released in Britain. Two weeks after release, it went to number one where it remained for nearly two months, selling 1.25 million copies in Britain alone. It was eventually knocked from the top slot by teen idol Peter Andre, Victoria's mother's favourite singer. During the endless rounds of interviews and TV appearances, the girls hardly had time to consider how they had come so far so fast. 'When I was little I always thought: "I want to be famous,"' said a rather perplexed Victoria at the time. 'But you could never dream of what's happened to us. It's a bit out of the ordinary.'

Indeed their boundless energy and joie de vivre seemed to capture a national mood. The girls were loud, proud and sometimes lewd and didn't seem to be afraid of anybody. As Mel B noted: 'The whole concept of Girl Power is about being aware of yourself, of not taking any crap from anyone and getting what you want. Not in a horrible way but in a nice way.' Politicians and prelates all used lines from the song's lyrics to make a point, whether it be about the economy or the health of the nation. Behind the aggressive can-do, sexually charged energy and attitude radiated by the group, were five down to earth suburban girls who loved their mothers and believed in traditional values; marital fidelity, the superiority of friendship with other girls to transitory male boyfriends and individual endeavour. When they proclaimed former Prime Minister Margaret Thatcher the original Spice Girl, they were speaking more accurately than they knew. 'They obviously have very clear political views,' said Conservative Central Office. 'They are a go ahead group and we are a go ahead party.'

In many respects, of all the Spice Girls, Victoria Beckham represents the creed of Girl Power. She is an archetypal suburban girl from the Home Counties; politically conservative, culturally disinterested and focused, almost obsessively, on home and family values. At the same time, while she was always dismissed as the least talented Spice Girl, in the longer run she has proved herself to be more disciplined, more cunning, more astute and ultimately more successful than the others. In a group defined by ambition itself, she has showed herself to be the most relentlessly ambitious.

After the success of 'Wannabe', the Spice Girls soon proved that they were not simply one-hit wonders. The hits simply came rolling out. In October 1996 their follow up single, 'Say You'll Be There', which so mesmerized David Beckham, took the charts by storm while their much-anticipated album trounced all competition in the Christmas charts. As Mel B recalled at the time: 'It's all happening so fast. One day we were no one, the next we were beating George Michael to number one.' They were dubbed 'Oasis in a Wonderbra' by *Smash Hits* magazine.

The pace was mesmerizing. Just five months after the world had first heard of them, they followed in the footsteps of royalty and Hollywood celebrity to switch on the Christmas lights in London's Oxford Street. Victoria's mother was the real star of the evening, spotting a young fan being crushed against a barrier and moving her to safety before the situation became too dangerous.

There was no let up. Even though they had taken Britain by storm they had to conquer America. With three number ones under their collective belts, the Spice Girls arrived in New York in January 1997 ready to do battle. The relentless schedule was beginning to tell. Victoria went down with flu but struggled through a host of personal appearances, interviews and photo shoots. Their hard work paid off; they stormed to the top slot in the all-important Billboard charts in February. Before they could draw breath they returned to Britain to perform the opening set for the Brit Awards at London's Earls Court. The year before they had come as nobodies, now they were fêted as pop royalty, nominated in five different categories. 'Things just seem to get better and better,' observed Victoria at the time. Their performance was a triumph, Geri's micro Union Jack dress stealing the show, especially when she revealed rather more of herself than had intended in front of an estimated 30 million TV audience. 'Everyone's seen them before so I don't give a damn,' she said later.

Still there was no let up. In March they sent themselves up for charity, their video of the hit single, 'Who Do You Think You Are?' being mimicked by celebrity lookalikes including the portly comedienne Dawn French who played Victoria. When she was trying to get into character, Dawn asked the famously po-faced Spice Girl why she never smiled. 'Because I get dimples,' came the reply. 'They make me look thirteen.' While the girls made publicity mileage from the video, in aid of Comic Relief, they were rapidly becoming the most marketable and marketed band in history. Their fans were able to buy an enormous array of merchandise, from Spice dolls, cameras, watches, lights, and books to videos and clothing. Then there were lucrative deals with, among others, Walkers crisps, BT phonecards, Polaroid, Cadbury's, Benetton, Pepsi Cola and Aprilia scooters, although the latter deal went wrong when Geri left, leaving the group with a substantial legal bill. Their video earned an estimated £5 million; they were paid £500,000 to launch Channel 5; while a personal appearance by the girls would cost upwards of £50,000. They weren't so much a pop group – after all they hadn't even done a live concert – more a recording and marketing phenomenon. As commentator Martin Samuel noted: 'Far from espousing Girl Power, what they appear to demand of their fans is meek consumerism.'

By now Victoria and the rest were multi-millionaires with all the trappings of superstardom; chauffeurs, secretaries, private jets, personal stylists, publicists and accountants. In the background orchestrating the whole show was the canny figure of Simon Fuller. Still there was no let up. After the singles and the videos, now there was the film, *Spiceworld:The Movie*. Billed as a madcap comedy, it took a light-hearted look at their lifestyle; the press conferences, rehearsals and concerts. They spent an exhausting six weeks filming, working from six in the morning until late at night, in various locations in London. Big name stars like Richard E. Grant, Lenny Henry and Elton John joined in the fun. The busy bandwagon rolled on. They appeared live in concert in Istanbul, Turkey, followed by a punishing tour of the Far East. Everyone was exhausted. The girls didn't have a life, they had a schedule and it was a gruelling one. They had been working for up to eighteen hours a day and even their brief holidays had been interrupted. Their manager controlled their every movement, their every action. When Geri pleaded for a week off, he refused and if any of the girls were in danger of being led astray he would move in to break up the

Right: Displaying precocious talent on the football field, David was a star player for Ridgeway Rovers in the Enfield District League.

Below: A youthful David Beckham makes his ambitions clear . . .

Above and right: David received a Manchester United replica shirt every year for Christmas from his father, so it was inevitable that he would inherit his fanaticism for the club.

Far right: David signed schoolboy terms with Manchester United on his 14th birthday before turning professional aged 16.

Above: David attends a film première in Bury in 1996 with his girlfriend, Julie Killelea, the daughter of a construction millionaire. She is now married to Manchester United defender Philip Neville.

Right: The Spice Girls – Victoria, Geri, Mel B, Mel C and Emma – pictured in July 1996, the month in which their first single 'Wannabe' was released – it reached the number one spot within two weeks.

Right: Victoria and Geri, performing 'Who Do You Think You Are?' at the Brit Awards, Earls Court, February 1997, where the Spice Girls triumphed, winning awards for Best Video and Best Single.

The Spice Girls look sensational in matching suits at the UK and US premières of *Spiceworld:The Movie*. In December 1997 in London they wore traditional British pinstripe. In Los Angeles in January 1998 they wore all white on the night.

Above: The Spice Girls and Prince Charles at a Prince's Trust concert held at Manchester Opera House in May 1997.

Right: Victoria embraces former South African President Nelson Mandela at a Prince's Trust concert held in South Africa.

Posh and Becks – the early days:

Left: Victoria visits David at his Manchester home.

Right: In January 1998 the worlds of music and football were united following the announcement of Victoria and David's engagement, only ten months after they first met. 'I could not be happier right now,' David told the world's media. 'I have my dream woman.'

Below: David and Victoria walk hand in hand.

Above: First home: the apartment block in Cheshire's desirable Alderley Edge. While the apartment is close to Old Trafford, it has never truly felt like home to Victoria.

Below: 'Beckingham Palace' on the Hertfordshire–Essex border. After extensive renovations David and Victoria will be settling in at the end of 2000. Victoria chose it as it is close to her parents' home in Goff's Oak.

Above left: A pregnant Victoria and David holidaying in Marbella, a few months prior to the birth of their son, Brooklyn. David was seen kissing her 'bump' in the Spanish resort.

Above right: Victoria attended various showbiz gatherings despite being heavily pregnant.

Right: Proud father: David leaves the Ivy restaurant in London. 'I love Brooklyn so much and I would do anything for him,' he has said. 'I'd recommend fatherhood to anyone.'

'His and hers' celebrity lifestyle:

Left: Dressed in matching black leather, David and Victoria attend the Versace Club in June 1999.

Right: The happy couple, prior to the much-fêted wedding in July 1999, pose for the cameras.

Below: David and Victoria at the MOBO Awards in London in October 1999.

Left: The 'New Royalty' have some fun taking delivery of their wedding thrones.

Below: The *Sun* newspaper puts a spin on the 'regal' nature of the Beckhams' fairy-tale wedding.

party. They were beginning to feel as if they were wrapped in cotton wool.

The harsh truth was that far from living the philosophy of Girl Power, the Spice Girls were effectively disempowered. They were living a lie and had been from the beginning. When the Spice Girls were launched, the idea was propagated that the all-girl group had done everything themselves. The legend was soon born that the can-do, can-have girls danced into the offices of Virgin's managing director Ashley Newton and spiced up his life. They performed a song and dance routine and he was immediately struck by their star appeal. He has said of the day that the girls gatecrashed their way into his life: 'When we saw them singing in our office we realized they weren't some pieced together vision by some male Svengali. They have their own agenda.' It was a refrain picked up by the girls themselves. 'We've had so many people say they managed us,' argued Melanie Brown. 'But we've all been in the music industry for years and we've done it ourselves. We do everything ourselves; we're completely into girl power and there's nothing us lot can't handle.'

In truth, as music critic Chris Blackhurst noted they were: 'an ersatz ensemble put together with the overriding purpose of making money for them and their backers. Behind those pouting poses, cheeky grins and Girl Power salutes, there is a programme of cynical media manipulation and calculating exploitation.'

They were a band put together by businessmen for the purpose of making money, not promoting sexual equality or liberation. As businessman Michael Sparkes admitted: 'I suppose you could say that they are all my own work. They were just put together like a piece of merchandise. I made their sound, their management company made their image.' Similar sentiments are shared by Ian Lee: 'I couldn't believe it when all these stories came out about how the girls did everything themselves. They are a put together band.' A male writer composing a feature on the Spice phenomenon dreamed up even their nicknames – Posh, Sporty, Ginger, Baby and Scary. Their first Svengali is more measured in his appraisal. 'It's true that I put the band together,' says Chris Herbert, 'but the girls always had their own energy and input. The way I describe it is that I put the ingredients together and the girls added the Spice.'

Everyone, from songwriters to publicists to the girls themselves, propagated the myth. For those at the centre, the Spice Girls themselves, it was hard to cope with the gulf between the image and the reality. During those days they used words like 'guilt' and 'feeling naughty' if they gave in to their true needs and desires. Melanie Chisholm took refuge in the gym; Victoria Adams in long phone calls to her family and later her boyfriend David Beckham. 'Sometimes it difficult when you are in America and all you want is a cuddle,' she said. On tour she became very homesick, crying every day because she wanted to return to her family. Home represented security, stability and a chance to be herself. For even her name, Posh Spice, was not really her character. While she liked designer clothes, she was a girl from the suburbs whose parents had earned their money by hard work and resilience. As Mel C says: 'She's not posh. She might wear posh clothes but she's as common as the rest of us.'

While they had money, acclaim and fame, the meetings with the great and the good, including Prince Charles and former South African President Nelson Mandela, they knew in their hearts that it had been achieved as much by the image makers and their manager as by their own endeavours. Like virtually every pop group before them, they wanted to be able to express themselves in their own way not only artistically but as individuals. They were tired physically and mentally as well as increasingly unhappy at the way their lives were simply out of their control. One source close to the group observed that the girls were exhausted and near hysteria. They had 'recently seen frightening symbols of their loss of power and control.'

In the beginning, when they were making their way, that had been acceptable; now the girls wanted a change of direction. They had enjoyed huge success very quickly, now they needed time to take stock and work out their future aims rather than simply being a money-making machine. Inevitably their thoughts moved towards a change in management. Matters were coming to a head. In the autumn of 1997,the leaders of the group, Mel B and Geri Halliwell, discussed the prospect of parting from Fuller. After the rigours of the Far East tour they felt that Victoria would agree. According to some accounts, Geri was allegedly angered by the friendship between their manager and the youngest Spice Girl, Emma Bunton.

Initially the girls, now fractious as well as worn out, discussed the delicate matter of splitting from their manager between themselves. Then they brought in their lawyers. In November 1997 while he was recovering from back surgery in London's Cromwell Hospital, the girls informed him that his services were no longer required.

A reported £10 million pay off sweetened the blow.

Although the band lost their extensive entourage and the back up provided by Fuller, they were winning back their lives. It was described in the media as the ultimate act of Girl Power. More accurately, it was the girls' first real enactment of their much-repeated slogan. 'I feel much more in control since we sacked our manager,' said Victoria. 'We're much happier doing it the way we're doing it now. Now we make our own decisions because that's the way we've always wanted it.' Similar sentiments were expressed by the other girls. Melanie Chisholm recalls that they had wanted to leave Simon Fuller's control for a long time but they had all felt too frightened. 'The day we left Simon was such a huge release for me,' she recalls. 'Until that day I'd feel guilty if I didn't go to the gym every day but now if I don't feel like going, I don't go and I don't care.'

It was a time for all of them to readjust, to sit down and think what stardom really meant for them. How could they do what they really, really wanted rather than dance to someone else's tune? In a way it was a story as old as pop itself. The tension between management and artiste, the differences between members of the group as they tried to do their own thing. The girls had been brought together by blind ambition, now they had a chance to see their way more clearly, to explore their innate talent. Ironically Fuller was fired just as the girls were voted best band in the world at the MTV awards in Holland. They had reached the summit of pop fame thanks to their guide and mentor. Now they wanted to reach for the stars on their own.

First indications were not good. Just a few days after the departure of Fuller, they seemed to suffer a collective fall from their platform boots. They were booed off stage during an awards ceremony in Spain because they asked photographers to leave, refusing to perform until they did so. The rumpus developed because the group fiercely protects its image to prevent anyone making money from selling pictures of them, but the timing was inconvenient to say the least. It is an added irony that at the centre of the row was the issue that had caused the split in the first place – control. Indeed it followed hard on the heels of a similar occurrence in India and another in Stockholm while Fuller was still in charge. At the same time first reports suggested sales of their second album in Britain and America were disappointing while *Spiceworld:The Movie* opened to less than ecstatic reviews. It looked as if public opinion was turning against the most marketed band in pop history. Everyone was waiting for the stars to fall to earth.

The critics were missing the point. If the girls were ever to find their feet, both creatively and as individuals, they would have to come back to earth. It would not be an easy process. Inevitably the tensions that they had experienced with their manager would soon re-emerge as infighting and bickering between themselves. Girl Power wasn't supposed to be like this.

Four

Queen
for a Day

THE sense of anticipation was almost palpable, the excitement at fever pitch. It may have been a grey, miserable March evening but those outside the unprepossessing Portland Hospital in central London knew they were part of celebrity history. The private hospital which had seen the arrival into the world of the Duke and Duchess of York's children, Princesses Beatrice and Eugenie, was the scene for another celebrity occasion. The birth of Brooklyn Joseph Beckham at 7.48 p.m. on March 4 1999 was greeted with the kind of fanfare normally granted a royal event. This was not just the birth of a child but the creation of a dynasty, Brooklyn the acknowledged heir apparent. His birth was by far and away the most famous of the 1,999 other babies born on that day and that evening it featured prominently on television news bulletins, knocking the bloody war in Kosovo off the front pages of tabloid newspapers. 'That really freaked me out,' observed Victoria. 'Anyone would think I'd given birth to a royal.'

Certainly the choreography bore all the hallmarks of a royal birth. First there came the official bulletin announcing that he was delivered by Caesarean section, weighed in at 7 pounds and was six days early. The waiting gaggle of camera crews, photographers, radio and print reporters as well as excited fans outside the hospital were duly informed that the proud father was in attendance and that mother and baby were doing fine. Naturally the footballer was 'over the moon' at his son's birth.

Then there was the arrival of the showbiz aristocracy, bearing gifts for the infant as he lay in his crib. The Spice Girls brought

balloons, champagne and flowers, Elton John sent a giant teddy
bear as well as a set of silver bowls from Tiffany while Donatella
Versace gave him designer baby outfits. Finally, after five days
resting in her private suite, it was expected that, like royal
parents, the happy trio would make a brief appearance so that
they could show the baby off to the world. Not this time. The
new House of Beckham had different ideas.

Instead David, Brooklyn and Victoria made their royal
getaway in a well-planned, high-speed operation. A limousine
with blacked out windows pulled up at the back entrance to the
hospital and seconds later sped off with an escort of police
motorcyclists acting as outriders, stopping traffic as the convoy
made their way to Victoria's parents' home in Hertfordshire. It
was if the elaborate security blanket covering the sleeping infant
seemed to signify that baby Brooklyn was in some ways even
more precious and protected than a royal prince.

As his parents were keen to make clear, his privacy was of
paramount importance. 'He's the one thing that is totally
private to us,' Victoria argued, 'He's not a money-spinner.' They
talked warmly about their love for their son, how David was the
perfect husband, changing nappies and feeding the youngster
and how Victoria could hardly bear to be away from the infant
for a second. The Beckhams were the perfect happy family,
doting on each other and their child, self-professed role models
for a generation. When the couple went out shopping they were
keen to protect him from intrusive photographers, shielding his
head with their hands.

Yet before he could utter more than a few words, Brooklyn
was one of the most photographed and talked about babies of
his generation, much of the coverage courtesy of his parents'
efforts. For much as the Beckhams protested about protecting
their son's privacy, he soon turned into a nice little earner for
them; he was only four months old when the first pictures
appeared in a magazine for money.

Indeed they were in the midst of financial negotiations for exclusive pictures for the most important event in their lives, their wedding, when Victoria discovered that she was pregnant. The couple, who negotiated a reported £1 million deal with celebrity magazine *OK!*, were surprised but thrilled by the news. 'It came at a perfect time in our relationship,' recalled Victoria who was on tour with the Spice Girls in America during the summer of 1998 when she realized that she was expecting a baby. He had been conceived during a crisis in David's professional career, the soccer star flying to join his fiancée in New York after his infamous sending-off during the World Cup. Hence the boy's name, relating to the district of New York where they had stayed during that fateful summer.

It was not the easiest of pregnancies, with Victoria having to appear on stage every night even though she suffered from chronic morning sickness. She joked that she would go through a dance routine, some of which were toned down because of her delicate condition, and then rush to the side of the stage to be sick.

During the hectic tour, made all the more stressful because of the abrupt departure of Geri Halliwell, she could hardly bear the sight of food, let alone eat it. Her morning sickness was compounded by her homesickness. America was a long way away from the alluring comforts of home. Comparing it with Europe, Victoria commented, 'I preferred the food in Europe, especially since you can usually find a Marks and Spencer there, and it does make a big difference when there's a huge time gap and you want to pick up the phone and ring somebody.' Her loneliness was magnified by the fact that David was in Britain during her tour, the couple keeping in touch through endless phone conversations.

Once she had come through the difficult early weeks, Victoria seemed to enjoy showing off her growing voluptuousness while David was a besotted father-to-be. He was seen publicly kissing her bump while the couple were on holiday in Marbella, Spain, talking with an uninhibited joy about fatherhood. 'I can't put into words what I feel for him; it's like a bond that started when he was in Victoria's stomach. It's unbelievable,' he said. There was talk that he had considered spending £100,000 on an ultrasound scanner to watch the baby grow inside Victoria and reports that they had a special twenty-minute home movie made of their unborn child whilst she was in America.

Yet all the money and technology in the world could not ensure that the baby would be born healthy. Like many mothers-to-be, Victoria was convinced there was going to be something wrong with her precious infant. A self-confessed born worrier, she fretted continually in spite of endless reassurance from her mother and David. 'It's something you have very little control over,' said the young woman who likes to be in charge of everything in her life.

At the very least she was determined to have total control over her wedding. It took fourteen months, hundreds of phone calls, letters, visits, and meetings to plan the event. Victoria and her mother Jackie masterminded the celebrity wedding of the year with a little help from a small army of assistants, organized by Peregrine Armstrong-Jones, the brother of Princess Margaret's former husband, Lord Snowdon. If the birth of Brooklyn marked the beginning of the Beckham dynasty, then the wedding represented their coronation.

The event, which took place on 4 July 1999, exactly four months after Brooklyn's birth, seemed to capture the spirit of Posh and Becks as individuals, a couple and a culture; a curious combination of childlike narcissism, conspicuous consumption and Disneyesque innocence. Billed as the wedding of the year, the sense of illusion and self-delusion was encapsulated in the fact that a couple, who publicly professed such intense love for each other, turned what is traditionally seen as a spiritual union into a photographic shoot. The abiding and certainly symbolic image of the wedding is of a weary David and Victoria huddled over a light box in the early hours of the morning, choosing photographs for the special issue of *OK!* magazine, when they should have been enjoying their first night together as a married couple. As profile writer Stuart Jeffries astutely observed: 'When *OK!* magazine devoted two issues to her wedding, it became disturbingly apparent how far she [Victoria] was prepared to go to bask in the public eye.'

It was a far cry from the romantic illusion of marriage Victoria held in her heart, an ideal expressed in the scrapbook of bridal pictures she had kept from her childhood. Once the couple had decided to marry she apparently took out her scrapbook and went through it ticking off wedding ideas that she had cherished since she was tiny. 'It will be her childhood dream come true,' a friend was quoted as saying.

The couple decided to theme their wedding on a fairytale because they believed they had a storybook romance and, as Victoria admitted, they were just big kids at heart. David lists as one of his hobbies tracing Disney cartoons and colouring them in. During their courtship he often faxed his efforts to Victoria adding a love note to the drawing. 'They have a lot of fun together too – he chases her around the house or they jump like kids on the bed, giggling and being generally soppy. They are very sweet together,' a friend observed.

But these were children who could afford to turn the world into a giant playground. They spent £500,000 transforming Luttrellstown Castle, an elegant eighteenth-century house outside Dublin, into a royal fairyland that owed more to Walt Disney than House of Windsor. It was themed à la Hollywood on the story of Robin Hood, the outlaw who steals from the rich and gives to the poor, the marquee and grounds decorated with greenery, twigs, apples, acres of velvet fabric in burgundy, dark green and cardinal purple as well as 15,000 fairy lights. They chose the theme music from the Disney cartoon *Beauty and the Beast* to make their grand entrance before the assembled throng and took to the dance floor to the strains of the theme from the movie, *The Lion King.* The grand finale of the evening was a spectacular four-minute firework display that would not have disgraced the Magic Kingdom itself.

As with every successful Disney production romantic and real royal history were combined. The genuine eighteenth-century chapel in the castle grounds, which was restored for the wedding, had enchanted Queen Victoria when she saw it during a visit in 1849. 'I do so wish Albert and I had married here,' the Queen admitted, moved by the sense of peace and tranquillity inside the small chapel. More than a century later, Victoria was equally entranced choosing the place, now named Queen Victoria's Folly, as the setting for the crowning event of her life. Royal jeweller Slim Barrett, who had worked with the late Diana, Princess of Wales, lent the bride a £100,000 diamond and gold coronet for her big day, the piece later being auctioned for charity.

These authentic royal connections were elaborated upon in the other arrangements for the day which were more reminiscent of Hollywood notions of royalty. The 255 guests, including the Spice Girls and Manchester United players, received invitations on parchment embossed with gold leaf and bearing a specially designed coat of arms with a swan, a crown and the words: 'Love and Friendship'. When they arrived at the imposing castle, it was indeed like a scene from the Magic Kingdom. A rich purple flag emblazoned with David and Victoria's crest and their initials fluttered in the breeze, a trumpet fanfare was played from the battlements while six-foot-long silk 'flames' shot from the castle turrets. Once safely inside the thick stone walls, the favoured few were given the imperial purple carpet treatment.

As they descended the impressive staircase to the banqueting marquee they were serenaded by liveried attendants in Irish costume. Afterwards they toasted the bride and groom from solid silver goblets, the newly-weds accepted their plaudits, holding court in his and hers red and gold thrones. Before the happy couple cut the tiered cake which was decorated with nude figures of David, Victoria and Brooklyn, the groom gave an insight into his wife's mindset and the dynamics of the relationship. 'I will always love and look after Victoria and treat her like a princess, because that's how she likes to be treated,' he told the guests.

This was a princess who liked to take command. She omitted the word 'obey' from the marriage vows, while David had meekly obeyed her wishes that he cancel his proposed stag night, and treat the wedding day as if he were in training for a big match.

Just as she gave the impression of controlling their partnership, so Victoria organized a wedding that was very much in their image. She left nothing to chance, calling Peregrine Armstrong-Jones five times a day. 'We knew what we wanted and discussed every detail with Peregrine. I could have left everything to him but I wanted to be hands on,' she said. The dress for instance, which was designed by American Vera Wang, took three transatlantic trips to New York for fittings for Victoria before she and her mother were satisfied with the £60,000 gown. 'It is very Scarlett O'Hara,' said Victoria.

On the big day, as David went for a relaxing round of golf, Victoria prowled the castle corridors, taking personal charge of last minute details. She gave three musicians from the eighteen-piece Starlight orchestra their marching orders because they 'didn't look right'. Like the rest of the band, the trio had been practising for six weeks beforehand. The last minute decision led to accusations that she was a 'nightmare control freak.'

Ultimately though beneath the sentiment and saccharine,

this was more than a wedding, it was an elaborate money-making scheme, not just for the Beckhams but the magazine that had paid a king's ransom for exclusive rights to the event. So guests, who were helicoptered in to avoid photographers lurking outside, suffered the indignity of being frisked for cameras before they entered the reception where no photography was permitted.

The proceedings crawled to a virtual standstill because of the demands of the official photographers, while dozens of security men and sniffer dogs patrolled the 560-acre grounds to keep out unwelcome media visitors. 'The main thing was that we wanted everyone to feel really comfortable and enjoy themselves,' said Victoria, without a trace of irony.

Naturally the whole affair attracted a battery of criticism not just because of the vulgar display, the royal pretensions and the conspicuous consumption but because the couple were cashing in on their romance, selling their wedding day. The fact that this is a regular practice among stars around the world was conveniently forgotten by those self-same critics. More interestingly when *she* discussed the couple's £1 million pay day, Victoria offered a telling insight into those values she holds dear. 'We wanted everything to be under control and to be safe,' she said on TV. 'The best way to do that was to have control over the pictures, the way they were taken, nobody pushing or shoving.' Those words again; control and safe, sentiments that seem to dominate her life.

Feisty yet sensitive to the merest hint of criticism, Victoria came out fighting to defend her fairytale wedding which was, as far as she was concerned, 'a dream come true'. The money spent and the decisions taken were a reflection of the couple's desires, as well as their sense of humour. 'A lot of stuff is tongue in cheek. We don't care what people say as long as we're happy and our families are happy, that's all that matters,' she protested, perhaps rather too vigorously.

For she might have been crowned a celebrity royal on her wedding day but she had yet to learn the age-old royal motto: 'Never complain, never explain.'

Five

Tears, Tantrums and Tenderness

I T had been a satisfying day for Victoria Beckham, her husband never far from her thoughts. For hours she and the former Take That singer Gary Barlow had been writing and recording love songs for her solo album in the hi-tech studios at his home in Cuddington, Cheshire, a few minutes drive from the Beckhams. The lyrics for the ballads she and Gary recorded all centred around her devotion and passion for David. By the end of the second long session she was feeling very pleased with herself, anxious to tell her husband how the day had gone.

She knew they had nothing special planned for that night; a Chinese takeaway maybe or an evening watching their favourite videos from the hit American sitcom, *Friends* or *Only Fools and Horses*. David had other ideas. It was May 2000, the end of a hectic soccer season, and with the League Championship in the bag, Sir Alex Ferguson had given him a six-day break. He wanted to do something special, something special for Victoria, the woman who had made his life so happy and fulfilled.

At first David, ever the romantic, had wanted to surprise her by flying her to an island she had always dreamed of visiting, Maui, near Hawaii, in the Pacific Ocean. But when he realized that it would take twenty-three hours flying time to reach this idyllic spot, he had to think again. Phone calls were made, friends and acquaintances sounded out. A senior executive from Virgin records, the Spice Girls' label, agreed to loan her secluded villa outside Florence in Tuscany, while another friend had a private jet standing by at Manchester airport to whisk the couple and baby Brooklyn away for their secret break in Italy.

All that remained was the packing. When Victoria left that morning for the thirty-five minute drive to Gary Barlow's mansion, David and her mother Jackie filled suitcases for the trip. Then David collected her from the singer's home, telling an unsuspecting Victoria that they had to drive to the airport to pick up a relative. It was only when she was about to board the flight to Tuscany that her husband revealed he was taking her on a second honeymoon.

His elaborate and expensive surprise is a sign of the profound love he feels for a woman he considers to be both his soulmate and his saviour, a partner who has helped to make him stronger and more self-aware. As he says: 'Victoria has given me so much confidence. I'm quite a shy person, but she's brought a bit more out of me.' Indeed, theirs is an almost obsessive love affair where they only come alive in each other's company. Their friend Rebecca Cripps observes: 'I have never come across such an all-consuming, powerful love.'

They regularly send short love notes and cards to one another, speak constantly on their mobile phones and buy each other small gifts. They are an intensely tactile couple, holding hands and cuddling each other in public, stroking and caressing each other in private. It's almost as though they live in a world of their own, sharing the same jokes, poking gentle fun at each other or just holding hands, Victoria absently stroking him as they talk. 'We love spending time together. We're both very affectionate and I've never really been like that with any other boyfriends,' says Victoria. These are not simply soundbite sentiments. In private and in public it is obvious they are a couple who have found themselves in one another.

On anniversaries and birthdays, David particularly makes a special effort. On Valentine's Day 2000, he got up early and filled their apartment in Alderley Edge with balloons, streamers and bouquets of lilies, Victoria's favourite flowers. Another time he rang singer Elton John to ask his advice on a piano he wanted to buy his wife as a surprise present.

He is equally given to extravagant, almost foolhardy, gestures that speak volumes about his devotion to the object of his affection. When Victoria was in Los Angeles on business he risked the wrath of his soccer manager by flying halfway round the world to spend two days with her. After paying for flights for himself, Brooklyn, his friend David Gardner and Gardner's girlfriend, Victoria's sister Louise, he had little change out of £20,000. While David was well aware that he could face trouble from his club – the couple flew back on separate flights to avoid adverse publicity – his romantic gesture made it clear where his priorities lay. He himself is in no doubt. As he says: 'Our relationship is the most solid thing in my life.'

On another occasion, returning from a soccer tournament in Tokyo, he did get permission from his manager to leave the rest of the team in order to surprise his new bride. Victoria was due to attend the Art of Barbie Ball with Elton John in aid of the singer's Aids Foundation. David arranged with Savile Row tailors William Hunt to make him a suit in the style of Barbie's boyfriend, Ken, to match Victoria's pink Barbie dress. The suit was made in double-quick time and biked to Goff's Oak to await his return.

As soon as he landed at Heathrow, David dashed to his in-laws' home, quickly washed and changed and drove to central London to be at his wife's side. 'It was a nice surprise to see David,' said Victoria, her matter-of-fact response revealing how much his thoughtful and romantic surprises are now an accepted part of their lives.

Yet theirs is a love that frequently sets off emotional fireworks. Their union draws its strength from an explosive dynamic of opposing emotions and priorities; her needy, him giving; her withholding, him generous; his gentleness, her aggression; his passivity, her dynamism; his romantic nature, her matter-of-fact qualities. The leader and the led: she the major breadwinner, he the house-husband; she the business-woman, he the child carer. In short, she Tarzan, he Jane.

Her boast that David is 'an animal in bed' and her belief that every woman in the world wants to snare her husband mask a deep and abiding insecurity. While her troubled soul may be the engine that has driven her relentless ambition, conversely her very outspokenness and her reflex aggression disguise a vulnerability which ensures she has not yet found peace of mind with her partner, no matter how often David reassures her or indeed how often she proclaims her love to the world.

She is aware of her emotional vulnerability, surges of anger rising within her if she sees another woman daring to look at her man. 'It makes me want to smack them in the mouth,' she has admitted. Her jealousy is exacerbated by the frequent physical distance between them, so that she frets and worries every time he is away on his own in Manchester.

No doubt she is particularly anxious when he goes out with his best friend, David Gardner, or with the Manchester United star Ryan Giggs. She must know all about their reputations for enjoying themselves and realizes that they could spell trouble for David. Indeed Victoria saw their effect on him at first hand when she and other Spice Girls went out on the tiles with David, Giggs and Gardner while they were recording their album in August 1999. Photographers noticed that David looked the worse for wear after an evening drinking tequila slammers with his friends in the fashionable Titanic bar and then in the Emporium nightclub.

The following morning a shamefaced David Beckham admitted that he had lost his diamond-encrusted wedding ring. No doubt Victoria was furious, not just because of the loss of such a sentimental possession but because of the influence Giggs and Gardner had had on him. Not that Victoria is much better when she is with her Spice Girl cronies. Their traditional drink is Asti Spumante, and as Victoria admits, it doesn't take much to make her squiffy. In the end a hotel cleaner found her husband's wedding ring, but the incident cannot have done much to improve Victoria's opinion of his friends – especially since David, when left to his own devices, has expressed his distaste for the laddish, boozy lifestyle of other young football superstars.

Any woman who chats up David when she is with him is likely to get the rough edge of Victoria's tongue – although she finds it highly amusing when gays come on to him. It is worse when they are in Manchester. On one occasion the couple were window-shopping in the Trafford Centre in Manchester when two young girls asked David for his autograph. The footballer, who was carrying Brooklyn, deposited him in his buggy and signed their books.

When the youngsters cooed over the baby, Brooklyn took this as his cue to burst into tears. The result was that Victoria accused David of being a bad father, asking him angrily why he was signing autographs for those 'tarts' in the first place. As sales staff and customers in the Clinton Card shop looked on in amazement the couple proceeded to have a heated exchange before marching out of the store to continue their verbal fisticuffs.

Her extreme, often irrational reactions must exasperate and bewilder a husband who is constantly expressing his love and devotion to his wife. Before he met Victoria, the soccer star had dated Julie Killelea, the daughter of a Lancashire construction millionaire, for two months. After they split up she started dating David's friend and fellow Manchester United player, Phil Neville. When they decided to get married in December 1999, the couple organized a colour co-ordinated wedding. They asked all the men to wear red ties with the initials P and J, for the twenty-three-year-old defender and his bride, while the female guests were requested to wear a combination of the team's red, white and black colours. Everyone obliged except for Victoria.

Determined to stand out on the bride's big day, Victoria stole the show in a strapless, low-cut, coffee-coloured designer dress split revealingly to the thigh. As one commentator noted: 'Posh Spice upstaged the bride.' Her behaviour did not endear her to the Neville family, not least because her outfit was widely featured in the pages of *OK!* magazine, which had paid £100,000 for exclusive rights to publish the photos of Phil and Julie's big day. The wedding itself took place in the same week that Victoria lost the stone from her own diamond ring during a shopping trip. She was frantic to ensure that she had a copy of the original to wear on the big day, fearing that if she appeared in public without her ring it would start tongues wagging. She appeared to be so wound up about the wedding of her husband's former girlfriend that it must have been something of a relief when a bomb scare at the reception, held at the Midland Hotel in Manchester, enabled her, David and Brooklyn to depart the wedding throng for a while before the all-clear was announced.

While her jealousy is the cross David has to bear, at times her suspicions have been justified. She was understandably furious when the press revealed that while she was in America touring with the Spice Girls in the autumn of 1998 David had been secretly dating a Page Three girl, Emma Ryan, from Stockport, Greater Manchester. They had gone out on a couple of dates and enjoyed late night chats on the phone, and he had even got her complimentary tickets for a home game. The tabloid tale of subterfuge, flirtation and romantic chatter confirmed all her worst fears about northern girls – and about David's dubious circle of friends. He had conducted his flirtation – the couple stopped short of an affair – with the connivance of one of them, Tim Bower, a fashion store manager.

David's embarrassing own goal was compounded by the fact that while he was secretly meeting the Page Three model, Victoria discovered that she was expecting a baby. In public Victoria announced that it was not a 'red card' offence, but in private she seems to have seriously considered sending him off. Rumours were rife that Victoria wanted to call off the wedding. No doubt it could not have been easy for either family to cope with the situation given the proximity of the ceremony and the lurid and very public description of his behaviour.

Often one of their spats is prolonged because of the distance between them. A tiff that would blow over in a matter of hours continues for days because one or the other has to go away on business. Invariably, during these emotional altercations, it is Victoria's mother Jackie who acts as the diplomat, soothing David out of a sulk or her daughter from an angry mood.

Nor is the jealousy and insecurity one-way traffic. David, who is very protective of his wife and who admits he has a short temper, would happily have confronted her former boyfriend Mark Wood when the latter was also present at the Brit Awards at Earls Court where the Spice Girls received their lifetime achievement award.

Such is David's possessiveness that Victoria, who is trying to build an acting career, knows that he would not condone it for a moment if she accepted a part that meant that she had to appear naked or in a nude love scene. Unfortunately, it would seem that to date these are the parts that most producers seem to think would be appropriate for her. Similarly, if Victoria has to go out alone to a showbiz event, her husband bridles if she decides to wear one of her many skimpy if glamorous outfits. He hates the idea of other men ogling her and there have been words between the couple about her fashion choices. From her point of view she feels that she can do and wear what she likes and, in any case, it was that glamorous look that attracted him to her in the first place. David worries about her revealing outfits, feeling that now they are married with a child, the flirty image that was so successful with the Spice Girls is no longer appropriate. As she admits 'I like short skirts, but David says I can't do that now I've got a baby.'

Not that David should ever have cause for concern. For all the raunchy dance routines and the sexy outfits, Victoria is a traditional, one-man woman who takes a dim view of those in her showbiz or soccer circle who stray from their partners. So she was shocked when a well-known TV personality chatted her up at a celebrity lunch, complaining primly afterwards about his behaviour.

Just as their mutual jealousy reveals how much they love and care for each other, so their wardrobes give an insight into the closeness of the bond that unites them. Both are performers who love the limelight, enjoying the adulation and acclaim. Their private selves are reflected in this public display, feeding the innate narcissism in their characters: Victoria the childhood show-off who loved to strike a pose, David the little boy who always liked to stand out and be different. 'I take pride in my appearance,' he says. Even as a child he had firm views on his image: once when he was a pageboy at a wedding, he chose to wear maroon velvet knickerbockers, long white socks and ballet shoes, even though his mother Sandra thought that he looked 'silly'.

David's dandyism has come to full flower since he met Victoria, sealing his reputation as a fashion icon and a gay pin-up. While Victoria has always been credited with shaping his style, it owes as much to his own theatrical instincts. Perhaps there is also a touch of rebellion against the old-fashioned values of his father Ted, who always mocks him when he sees pictures in the media showing David, now known as Camp David, in his famous sarong or wearing a silk bandana. As far as his father is concerned, football comes first, second and last in life; fashion is an effeminate distraction. He reportedly told a friend: 'Just look at him . . . it's not the David I know.'

From the moment David saw Victoria dressed head to toe in PVC for a pop video and she spotted the Manchester United player in the pages of a glossy magazine, they hunted each other out as assiduously as any big game trophy-hunter. Once captured, these two young people saw in each other a reflection of themselves, their vanity and self-absorption perfectly matched. As the relationship has developed they have become almost interchangeable; their mannerisms, their body language and particularly their clothes have become remarkably similar.

It started with the famous matching purple outfits for their wedding in Ireland and soon became a signature that defined the couple. So for a Gucci party they wore identical leather outfits, for a night out at the trendy Sugar Reef restaurant they were in matching denim while for a film première they were in similar brown gear. Hailed as style icons, there is an androgynous sexuality about their behaviour, a quality that might explain their popularity with the gay community.

However there is a danger inherent in an existence where Posh and Becks as a couple are seen as a brand, an institution and a lifestyle. As marriage guidance counsellor Lucy Selleck of Relate warns: 'If people's identities are too linked into "the couple" rather than themselves that could be a problem. We call such couples Babes in the Wood. They cling to each other in an unhealthy way and can't function properly.'

Like the real royal family, there is an 'us against the world' quality about their behaviour, giving each other mutual support during some of the very public traumas in their lives. When David was sent off during the World Cup, it was to Victoria he turned for comfort and consolation. In a neat role reversal, it is she who tells him he looks 'lovely' in an outfit because for all his pin-up good looks he is often unconfident about his appearance.

Again it is she who goes out and publicly defends him against critics who suggest that he is 'thick', with a voice like a vacant little boy. She is desperately concerned to set the record straight on his behalf. Crucially, while it rankles with her what the rest of the world thinks, he professes not to care. 'Victoria gets more annoyed than I do about people saying I'm thick and that I sound stupid. I just get on with it,' he says.

When one of his childhood friends committed suicide, David was devastated by his tragic death. As youngsters they had played soccer together and David had kept in touch with him when he left to play in Manchester. Victoria, knowing that it was the first time her husband had attended the funeral of a close friend, showed a maturity few would credit, mothering him solicitously through his ordeal.

Equally, David shows the same intense concern for Victoria. Before a game, if he knows she is in the crowd, he scans the stadium to make sure she is all right. Only then does he relax and play football. Sometimes he takes his support for her to extremes. During the last Spice Girls tour he sat in the front row night after night even though he knew that the first five rows would be drenched in fake snow which showered that part of the audience. After a few nights most fans brought umbrellas, but not David. He insisted on sitting in the same seats without protection.

He is doubtless the first to console her if there is an unpleasant press item about her. Instinctively aware of her vulnerability and emotional uncertainty, he endlessly bolsters her self-esteem, complimenting her, for example, about a new album track she has laid down. Indeed she is so needy of his support that they had a disagreement when he failed to ring her soon enough after she had sashayed down the catwalk during her first attempt as a model. It was a short-lived tantrum, for they were soon billing and cooing over each other, but it shows just how much she relies on his reassurance.

The episode illustrates an essential difference between the couple. He seems content to be who he is, secure in his skin, a talented footballer doing what he has always wanted. On the other hand Victoria is driven by the demons within; a woman who is at once dauntless, intrepid and dynamic and yet insecure, vulnerable and needy.

Certainly the question of talent is an issue. David has innate ability while Victoria made her fame and fortune through hard work, determination, drive – and a large slice of luck. 'He gets more respect because he is more talented,' she has noted, a view that reflects the common belief that she is the weakest singer in the Spice Girls, the one known for her looks rather than her voice. In the ephemeral world of showbiz that knowledge breeds its own insecurity. As consultant psychiatrist Paul Flowers observes: 'While she has a lot of acclaim she feels that she is a bit of a fraud, famous for being famous. So when she is with her contemporaries and peer group, that is, other singers and showbiz types, she may feel that she is something of a failure. Fame is a hollow achievement and having struggled and strived for success, once she has attained that goal she may feel more, not less, insecure.'

So while Posh and Becks are both vain and self-absorbed, almost inevitable qualities in lives performed so publicly, it is Victoria whose constant craving for attention leads her to the wilder shores of excess. She is a past master at producing the outrageous remark. The constant need to make headlines means there is never a question, however personal, that she will not answer, a statement she will not make.

She announced on her official web site, for instance, that she 'crouched to avoid contact' when it came to toilet hygiene. She also boldly revealed that 'I've weed in front of David right from the beginning, but then we've always been more like friends.' She is forthright about motherhood – 'I've given up breast-feeding now,' she said, explaining how 'Brooklyn was getting too hungry, so I'm feeding him bottles. My nipples didn't get sore or anything. I just wasn't giving him enough,' – and when asked by the men's magazine *GQ* if she had ever been totally sexually satisfied she said: 'Yes, recently. That's important if you want to spend the rest of your life with someone – if not you start to look elsewhere.'

Nor was this an isolated comment. As she enthusiastically told showbiz writer Dominic Mohan: 'I want another [baby], that's for sure, but we are both so busy. That's not to say our sex life isn't great though.' Then she added, some would say over defensively: 'It's fantastic and always has been, thank you very much.' As the novelist Shyama Perera noted: 'It's as if she thinks a constant public acknowledgement of their union will provide the spiritual underpinning for their love.'

Her frankness about their personal life contrasts with David's demeanour, a young man who treads warily when he is on parade, saying little in public and giving away less. Of course it must be remembered that as an international footballer David's name makes the sports headlines on an almost daily basis, Victoria has to work harder to grab the spotlight. Nowhere was this better expressed than during Channel 4's *The Big Breakfast* when she remarked that her husband had worn her thong underwear, a seemingly throwaway line which was none the less guaranteed to make headlines in the tabloids.

Interestingly it was Victoria herself who later underlined the absurdity of anyone taking this story seriously in an interview with *Evening Standard* columnist Zoe Williams. 'I mean, how's he going to fit into one of my thongs?' she pointed out.

A perfectionist, she has known from an early age that she has had to try harder and work harder if she want to reach the top. With little God-given talent, it is her determination and ferocious self-belief that has sustained her. She is a born leader who commands respect, and at times fear, from those who cross her. Victoria has often said that she is the 'bitch' while David is the 'pussycat'. The celebrity photographer Annie Liebovitz captured the essence of her dominance and his docility during a photo shoot in a Scottish baronial mansion where she had the couple striking rather smouldering if self-conscious poses, the mistress of the manor and the sensual servant.

Victoria is the business brains of the partnership, the one who thinks up schemes and organizes deals, exploiting their celebrity to the full. Dynamic and aggressively ambitious, no doubt she becomes frustrated by his seemingly more laid back, easygoing nature. It is something of an illusion. Her restless energy points to deep-seated anxieties, tensions manifested in her eating habits and the very public debate about her weight loss. The woman who can make David Beckham laugh one minute and cry the next is much more troubled than she or her circle would like to admit.

While the arrival of her first child Brooklyn in March 1999 gave her and David a completion of sorts, the baby also acted as a counterpoint to many of the issues in her life that she has yet to come to terms with, issues that stem from her perfectionist personality and her childhood. Not for nothing is her company called Moody Productions.

Six

A Bridge Called Brooklyn

I T was a family outing to the zoo that would have had photo-graphers purring with delight. There was the nation's number one heart-throb, stripped to the waist, clinging to the bars of the lions' cage. As he flung lumps of red meat to the prowling big cats, his son Brooklyn watched with obvious adoration at the antics of his macho father. In the background, David's mother-in-law Jackie Adams took pictures for the family scrapbook while Victoria, Tony Adams, his sister-in-law Louise and her toddler Liberty looked on.

Based in the grounds of the Paradise Wildlife Park in Broxbourne, near the Adams family home in Hertfordshire, the zoo had closed off the lion enclosure to give their celebrity visitors a chance to enjoy themselves in peace and privacy; however, David must have felt some uneasiness.

By being away from his home base in Manchester, just before he and his team-mates were due to fly to Italy for a match against Valencia in the European Cup, David was knowingly flouting club rules, and risking the wrath of his manager, Sir Alex Ferguson. Both his parents, especially his father who has earned the respect of Ferguson for the loving commitment and sacrifice he has shown throughout his son's career, will have been concerned to point out to him the importance of remaining in the manager's good books.

There were other reasons for concern and perhaps dismay. Ted and Sandra Beckham dote on their grandson, but feel that they do not see him often enough, and so they would probably

94

have regarded the Sunday afternoon trip, in March 2000, as another missed opportunity to spend time with the toddler. The day out with his in-laws will have been viewed as another example of the growing influence of Victoria's family on their son, straining the already uneasy relationship between the two families. Ever since his marriage, his parents have constantly worried about the emotional and physical demands made of their son as he tries to reconcile his football career in Manchester with the showbiz lifestyle favoured by Victoria and her family. While Ted Beckham has hinted at the tensions, he has tried to smooth over talk of a rift. 'Of course we have differences, the same as anyone else,' he has said. 'I'm from a footballing background, they are from a music background, but we have a good relationship with them.'

Their fear that the Adams family will affect David's performance on the pitch may reflect a deeper concern that they will never be able to compete with the opulent and glamorous lifestyle of their high-profile in-laws. In private Ted has spoken to friends about the fact that David's personality and ideas seem to be changing, not always for the better.

While the Adamses live in a detached mock-Tudor mansion in leafy suburbia, and drive round in Rolls-Royces and Porsches, the Beckhams make do with a modest semi-detached house in Chingford, Essex. David's father works long hours as a commercial kitchen fitter, partly so that he can earn enough to enable him and his wife, who is a part-time hairdresser, to watch their son play every week, be it home or abroad. Inevitably though, they may feel overshadowed by the Adamses, a sense that they are second-class citizens in the new world of Posh and Becks. They may have gained a daughter-in-law, but they might also feel that they are losing a son.

It was at the lavish wedding that the first cracks appeared between the two families. Although the bride's family is traditionally responsible for the wedding plans, it was natural that Ted and Sandra would have wanted to be involved in the organization of their son's wedding, but they were sidelined. Victoria and her mother Jackie decided the venue, the flowers, the caterers and the entertainment. Like many commentators, members of the Beckham family felt the celebration was extravagant and wildly over the top. David's uncle Peter, who was left off the guest list, observed: 'The lavish display didn't fit in with what I know of David. It's probably Victoria's influence not David's.'

Perhaps more hurtful was the impression left by David in his speech at the wedding in which he seemed to spend more time praising the Adamses than his own family. Indeed this may help explain some of the difficulties facing the two families. According to marital etiquette he was correct to behave in this way but the Beckhams, feeling rather upstaged and marginalized, may have felt, once again, that they were being downgraded. From that time slights, real or imagined, have dogged the relationship, particularly with Victoria.

The most public manifestation of this ill-feeling took place at the wedding of David's sister Lynne at a register office in Hornchurch, Essex in October 1999. There was keen anticipation that Brooklyn would be present and so everyone felt let down when he was not brought along to the event. Victoria's absence was also significant. As onlookers shouted, 'Where's Posh?', newspaper commentators saw her lack of presence as a sign of a family rift.

While one spokesperson for the Spice Girl said that she had been up with the baby all night, another said that she was recording in Sheffield. The bride and the rest of the Beckham family could be excused for feeling confused by these contradictory explanations.

As with many families, money is a point of division. In any argument about cash, Victoria will be able to remind David that, even though he is a multi-millionaire, she earns three times more than he does. That financial disparity has been made apparent on a number of occasions when they have splashed out on their respective families. So Tony Adams celebrated his 53rd birthday with a Porsche Boxster car, courtesy of Victoria and David while Ted Beckham received a Manchester United shirt with his son's name on the back. Again Victoria spent £500,000 on a house for her sister and brother next door to their parents compared with the more modest semi in Ilford, Essex, that David bought for his sister Lynne. When Lynne was given a new Ford Escort, Louise Adams received a more expensive A-class Mercedes and Victoria's brother got a new Golf GTI convertible. An exception to the inequality in their generosity was the gift of a Mercedes tied with a red bow that Ted received for Christmas.

While David and Victoria have every right to spend their money exactly as they choose, it is entirely understandable if the Beckham clan felt somewhat aggrieved by the disparity.

More than money, the birth of Brooklyn has come to symbolize the tensions between two such close-knit, supportive, yet very different families. The Beckhams are a demonstrative and very loving family, deeply protective and justly proud of their superstar son and equally adoring of their grandson. 'What I really liked was that David was really close to his family,' recalls Victoria of her first encounter with the Beckham brood. So if there is a chance of seeing his grandson, Ted will finish work early for the opportunity to spend time with him. As a doting grandfather, he loves to roll around on the floor with the toddler, tickling him and playing games, invariably something involving a ball.

When Victoria and David are preoccupied with business matters, Sandra is only too happy to look after Brooklyn. She feeds and plays with him, reading him books and taking him for walks in the local park. She has even been seen giving him hamburger and ice cream at the local Burger King in Chingford. As a mother of three children and something of a surrogate mum, she naturally enjoys Brooklyn's company and she and her husband always look forward to the times they can spend with him. As David is nearby at the Adams' house at Goff's Oak so frequently, there is often a deep sense of disappointment when they miss seeing the youngster for some reason or another.

Although David's parents may not see their son and grandson as much as they may wish, it is beyond dispute that they are proud of the way he has taken to fatherhood. His behaviour is a reflection of the loving and caring environment in which he was brought up. In David, it has brought out a nurturing, protective and publicly demonstrative love that has seen him hailed as a New Man, a model father for a new generation. Indeed psychologist Professor Anthony Clare has argued that the football star is even more preferable as a role model than the Prime Minister Tony Blair, who became a father for the fourth time at the age of 46. He has said: 'Beckham is a better example because football is such a male environment. The fact that he is prepared to be so involved with his baby really matters to all the young men who want to be affectionate to theirs but have no role models. Those England fans wouldn't have taunted him about his baby before, because it wouldn't have been seen as part of him that really matters.'

In public and private, David is the personification of the doting father, spending every minute he can with his son. As Beckham says: 'I love Brooklyn so much and I would do anything for him. I'd recommend fatherhood to anyone. If I've had a bad day or I'm getting stressed about something, it's wonderful to come home and see him. It just clears my mind and I forget about everything.'

He loves feeding him, watching him breathe, loves witnessing the almost daily changes in his appearance and even enjoys changing his nappies. During the football season he takes him to training at Manchester United's new practice centre at Carrington, leaving him in the players' lounge where the toddler plays happily with a toy dog, watched by adoring canteen staff. Even on match days the youngster is never far from his thoughts. After the half-time team talk during home games at Old Trafford David pops into the crèche to snatch a few moments with his son.

Now that Brooklyn is walking – the couple like to video every move he makes – he is able to kick a miniature ball with his dad who waits for the day when he can enjoy a real kick-about with his son like other United player fathers. When he and Victoria looked at Heath Mount, the £2,335 a term prep school in Hertfordshire proposed for Brooklyn, they were shown around by headmaster the Reverend Harry Matthews. David was doubtless nonplussed to learn that the school only played rugby. However, having a superstar dad to teach the boys the tricks of the trade must be a strong incentive to put football on the syllabus.

While he has worn golf shoes emblazoned with his son's name, perhaps his most public statement of affection was the guardian angel tattoo he had etched between his shoulder blades with 'Brooklyn' tattooed to the base of his spine. 'Brooklyn is beneath so it's like he's watching over him,' David said afterwards. The design, which was inspired by an album cover of his favourite rap artist 2Pac, took two hours to etch in and the pain of the operation left the soccer star with tears in his eyes. Tattooist Louis Molloy, who spent two weeks researching the design based on David's initial sketch, observed: 'David did say that it hurt but hats off to him he stuck with it and took it.' Indeed it was so painful that David's friend Gary Neville, who had considered having a tattoo, decided that it was not for him.

After the initial tattoo work, David and Victoria were said to have spent several evenings looking through a book of Latin quotations to find a suitable inscription to put under the outstretched arms of the guardian angel. In the end they chose

'*Et Animus Liber*' (Free Spirit), but after the pain of the initial tattoo, David has been reluctant to enter Molloy's Manchester tattoo parlour again.

Less macho but more fun, David loves to take Brooklyn to the weekly meeting of Tumbletots, a playgroup for pre-school children. He joins in with the toddlers and their mothers singing nursery rhymes such as 'Row, row, row your boat', or watches Brooklyn as he dives through hoops on the junior assault course or plays in the 'pond' filled with plastic balls.

When the couple first arrived at the Old Masonic Hall in Macclesfield, the local Tumbletots venue, mothers were agog that the new royal family had deigned to join them. They had been told beforehand not to take photographs or ask for autographs and to treat them as they would any other newcomers. Tumbletots organizer Martin Lawson recalls: 'Brooklyn is fabulous. No problems. A smashing little boy.'

As Brooklyn, who is developing a sunny, jolly personality, really enjoyed playing with the other children, they decided to make it a regular event although it is David, rather than his mother, who takes him to the Tumbletots centre in Bramhall, Manchester. At first he was rather embarrassed and self-conscious, not only because he was the only man there but because his celebrity status had put him in the spotlight amidst the fifteen or so mothers who spent their time watching him when they thought he wasn't looking. For once Victoria was amused by their behaviour rather than jealous of it. She said: 'He loves spending any time he can with him. That's what you do with kids – and we appreciate every second.'

David is so besotted with the youngster that when he comes home late from a game or a night out he often wakes Brooklyn up to play with him, treasuring every moment of quality time they spend together. Their son appears to accompany them everywhere – a diner at the fashionable Ivy restaurant was surprised when Victoria lifted a sleeping Brooklyn out from under the table. He is likely to be taken out of his cot at all hours of the day or night for a long motorway commute or for a plane flight.

They are typical parents with everyday concerns and fears for their young child but with extraordinary means at their disposal. Their wealth and celebrity enables them to charter jets at a whim but doesn't protect them from ordinary cares and woes. Moreover it makes them even more protective parents, the ever-present paparazzi and the very real threat of kidnap constantly on their minds.

It means that the normal events of childhood – a walk in the park, a day trip, even a birthday party – can no longer be taken for granted. Formerly simple leisure activities have taken on a more complex nature.

Fearful of being photographed or followed, Victoria and her baby are often prisoners in their penthouse apartment in Alderley Edge. They don't mix with the neighbours in their complex, rarely use the communal lawns or go for a stroll to give the boy a breath of fresh air in the nearby parks. The couple's fear of stalkers is no celebrity chimera. A mentally deranged woman bombarded the soccer star with love notes and sent items of clothing to his apartment.

Then she took to sitting outside on a bench nearby watching for any sign of the footballer. On one occasion she ran up to his car when he was waiting for the electronic gates to open and shouted: 'I love you, I love you.' Even a visit from the police failed to put a stop to the harassment. A few days after the police had seen her, she tried to enter the building to speak to the object of her fixation but got no further than the ground floor. In the end the police were forced to detain her under the Mental Health Act.

While that was an extreme and very unnerving series of events, the couple also receive unpleasant and threatening mail on quite a regular basis. There was even an incident where the brake pipes of David's Ferrari sports car were allegedly cut by an unknown assailant.

In the Beckhams' world of hype and unreality, where truth and fiction seamlessly blend, serious commentators found it hard to assess the truth in the alleged act of sabotage, especially as the story made front-page news on the eve of Victoria's solo single release. The publicity surrounding the attempt to snatch baby Brooklyn outside Harrods occurred just before David appeared in court to argue that the 'special circumstances' of his celebrity lifestyle demanded that a driving ban be lifted.

As the death threats and deranged stalker have proved, it cannot be denied that the Beckhams do face genuine dangers and so have to exercise due caution and wariness. Consequently, rather like real royalty, anything they do has to be orchestrated and organized. Spontaneity is the first casualty in the world of super celebrity. So when they decided to take Brooklyn to Stockley working farm near Knutsford in Cheshire last spring, the farm manager was contacted and warned that the Beckhams were coming. With security staff in tow to keep away onlookers, the couple spent a happy few hours looking at the farm animals. Brooklyn, who loves dogs, was mesmerized by a giant sow while Victoria enjoyed cuddling a newborn lamb. Farm manager Richard Furnace said afterwards: 'They were approachable, not at all aloof and interacted with the animals.'

While visitors to the farm were delighted when the Beckhams signed autographs afterwards, it was a different story when they took Brooklyn to Chester Zoo on Victoria's twenty-sixth birthday. Even though they requested a private day out, photographers were on hand to snap them as they strolled around in between heavy rain showers. Over-protective zoo staff then closed the monkey house and giraffe enclosure to the paying public so that their celebrity guests could enjoy a few minutes privacy. It did not please the public who were left out in the rain, nor were the local chamber of commerce impressed.

Secretary Bob Clough-Parker thought it was a 'bit rich' for a couple enjoying their celebrity status to complain of media attention.

While the Beckhams received a few media brickbats, that operation was literally a stroll in the park compared to the commotion surrounding Brooklyn's first birthday party. That really was a zoo as Press and public converged on a Knutsford hotel that Victoria had chosen to turn into a circus for a day. Before the clowns, the tumblers, stilt-walker and the face-paint artists arrived for the £10,000 party, the rooms were prepared as if for a high-powered political summit. Former soldiers turned security men swept the place for bugs and hidden cameras before watching stony-faced as an array of guests including Manchester United players and Spice Girls arrived to join in the fun. They formed a phalanx of grey suits to stop photographers taking pictures of the activities inside, including cutting the birthday cake.

The event illustrated the mixed and confusing signals which David and Victoria send out about their treasured son. It is an incongruous combination of protection and exhibitionism. Whilst they fear for his life and privacy, shielding his head from photographers for example, they dress him from top to toe in designer clothes, parade him round like a trophy and sell family pictures. Just as her mother pushed Victoria into a modelling agency, so Victoria now wants Brooklyn to have a modelling career, his face appearing on the cover of glossy magazines like Vogue. 'He loves all the attention he gets. He's a real exhibitionist,' she says, qualities obviously inherited from his mother. Victoria's role as mother is characterized by this ambivalent behaviour – on the one hand showing off about her son, and on the other being intensely protective of him.

For while the birth of Brooklyn has brought joy into the lives of his parents, his arrival has awakened contradictions that have lain beneath the surface of their personalities. It has been a rather confusing journey for Victoria, his birth provoking a personal psychological battle. His arrival could have forced her to confront difficult emotional issues which are seated in her relationship with her family, particularly her mother, and in her own resolute, highly-disciplined nature. This conflict is illustrated by her considerable weight loss since the birth of Brooklyn. This has been seen by many, including psychologists, to indicate that she may suffer from an eating disorder.

Indeed it is worth returning to her childhood to find clues to understand her behaviour. The Adamses are the ultimate tight-knit, closed family who have deliberately set themselves apart from others, their independence bolstered by their reliance on one another. As youngsters Louise, Victoria and Christian were discouraged from leaving the family compound to play with other children. Victoria's own memories are of her father's long hours, the chaotic mealtimes and her own unpopularity at school. She was famously singled out as different when her father dropped her off in his Rolls-Royce.

Her school life was a hostile counterpoint to her time at home. 'I was picked on a lot at school. I was never particularly good at anything at school but I had a lot of drive and ambition. I didn't have a nickname because nobody would talk to me.'

When those outside were the enemy and equalled unhappiness, it is not hard to see where she inherited her chippy 'me against the world' attitude as well as her seeming indifference to public opinion. 'I'm not that desperate to be liked,' she says.

However there were other qualities that helped her on the path to fame and fortune. The tough-minded drive and business acumen that brought Tony and Jackie Adams to leafy suburbia from the streets of Tottenham in north London was echoed in the ambitions they harboured for their offspring. Jackie registered all three children with a modelling agency and for a time Louise was more successful than her elder sister.

Like anyone involved in the image business, Victoria

naturally cared more about how she looked and appeared than perhaps her teenage contemporaries. As an erstwhile model and as a drama student with dreams of a career as a dancer or singer, this merely served to emphasize her concerns about her poor skin and insecurity about her figure.

At the same time she is refreshingly honest and open about her natural appearance. As she says: 'I look terrible most of the time. I'm not one of these people who can get out of bed and look great, like Natalie Imbruglia. I imagine that she looks great all the time but I'm not like that.'

Yet when she found fame with the Spice Girls, looks counted for a lot. Her image as the pouting, classy flirt was carefully controlled by her manager, Simon Fuller. For a young woman who likes to be totally in command it brought about something of a conflict, even though she liked the look. Like the other Spice Girls the other thing she did not have complete control over was her body and her diet. As Mel C has said the decision to break with him was a 'huge release' as they stopped feeling guilty about what they ate and remembered who they really were as individuals. She recalls: 'I went completely teetotal and would never, ever eat anything naughty. Now I am in control of my life, I've loosened up a bit and even have a drink now and then. Now it's like, so what?'

The underlying unhappiness she felt, even at the height of her success, meant that for Victoria security and safety resided in her home life. Even though she left home after leaving school to attend theatre college, Victoria is a self-confessed home bird. When she found fame with the Spice Girls, she was the one who was truly homesick on tour, endlessly phoning her mother and father for comfort and advice. It is easy to see why. Her father is very protective of her well-being, easily provoked to aggressive behaviour by the presence of paparazzi photographers when he is with her in public. Even though her mother Jackie is easygoing and welcoming on the surface, like her husband, she is as protective as a lioness looking after her cubs when it comes to her children. She has no hesitation in complaining to the media if she feels that they have unjustly criticized her daughter.

Now twenty-six, Victoria is a curious amalgam of confident superstar and little girl who has yet to cut mummy's apron strings. It is a relationship of mutual dependence where both mother and daughter seem to have moved on little since the days when Victoria was a schoolgirl. Victoria, who bought the house in Sawbridgeworth because it was near her parents, seems lost and alone when she is at the Alderley Edge apartment, and returns to her parents' house as often as possible. There is a certain symbolism in the fact that she occupies the same bedroom as she did as a child. Her reluctance to fly the nest has so far proved expensive, her husband being fined at least £100,000 by his soccer manager for behaviour caused in part by his lifestyle as a long-distance commuter.

This is the contradiction in her life. For all too often she is more than happy to be cosseted, her every need and whim taken care of by her mother, be it looking after the baby, washing and ironing her clothes or taking care of day to day decisions. At the same time both her mother Jackie and her younger sister Louise act as her personal assistants, religiously saving every single picture and press cutting, making diary arrangements and sorting out the accounts.

While the other Spice Girls have engaged the services of professionals, Victoria relies only on her immediate family. As her sister Louise says: 'I'm the only person she can trust.' While Victoria controls the purse strings and access to a glamorous world, it is all too easy to imagine how this has altered the emotional dynamic inside the family, mother and sister behaving rather like ladies-in-waiting, dancing attendance on a princess. They have become used to her wildly varying moods, one minute equable, the next depressed and snappy.

This contrast between the way Victoria likes to project herself as an independent young woman in control of her life and a private world where she is less certain and confident was made manifest with baby Brooklyn. During her pregnancy she was a perfect example of the new breed of celebrity women like Madonna, Demi Moore and Mel B who were proud to be pregnant. They celebrated their womanhood and unborn child, wearing skimpy outfits that showed off their bulge or, as with actress Demi Moore, appeared naked on the covers of magazines. Their bulges were beautiful, not something to hide away under voluminous outfits.

So Victoria and David happily posed for pictures when she was highly pregnant, the mother-to-be talking in no-nonsense, practical tones about how she was going to bring up her child, speaking confidently of not hiring a nanny, of taking the infant into the recording studios in a backpack and bringing him up in a down-to-earth manner. 'Straight in the cot, because you have to draw the line somewhere although I have heard there are some babies who never sleep . . . aren't there?' She was constantly keen to assert both in words and deeds that she was in control of her pregnancy, in control of her life, indeed in control of her future.

As with so many other aspects in her life, there was a contradiction between the talk and the practicalities, the strong projected image and the uncertain reality. Her idealized notion of life with Brooklyn came down to earth with a bump in the months after he was born – much as many mothers had predicted. As mother Louise Young observed: 'We've all given fish-eye looks to first-time pregnant women who sport charming naivete. Have they ever noticed that babies squeak when you put them down? Does she know that as soon as you've dressed babies, they crap? As soon as you've changed them, they're hungry. As soon as you've fed them, they need winding. As soon as you've winded them they're sick? I predict rude awakenings. Possibly several times a night.'

Sleepless nights and constant worry was indeed the reality for Victoria who, like millions of mothers before her, discovered the difference between great expectations and the mundane reality. Not that Brooklyn was the easiest of babies in the early months. When he was just two months old, Victoria held his hand and cuddled him as he was given a general anaesthetic before a hernia operation. The couple admit it was the most upsetting thing they had ever gone through, naturally worried about their son during his hour-long operation at the private Portland Hospital in London. Besides his hernia from which Brooklyn effected a full recovery, he has suffered from all the usual childhood ailments, and he is particularly prone to ear infections, not surprisingly given his jet-set lifestyle.

More worrying for his parents has been his apparent inability to hold down his food, a condition that famously caused him to be sick over his father's suit on his wedding day.

Victoria confesses that she is a 'paranoid' mother, always worrying about the health of her 18-month-old son. In the early months she would often go into Brooklyn's bedroom in the night and put a mirror next to his mouth to check that he was still breathing.

When the singer, who helped launch a national meningitis campaign, heard that her sister's daughter Liberty was running a high fever, a symptom associated with the killer illness, she may well have suspected the worst. Fortunately, the youngster only had a minor ailment and quickly recovered.

Just as her brave talk before the birth contrasts with her private difficulties, so her boast that she does not need or want a nanny is not quite what it seems. In spite of her busy and demanding schedule Victoria is adamant. 'I insist on being with him every step of the way,' she says. 'I know people think it's weird that we don't have a nanny but we insist on doing everything ourselves. People think it's funny but we wouldn't have it any other way.'

The reality is that without the continual support of her husband and her extended family, as well as advice from friends like Mel B, whose child is a month older than Brooklyn, and mother of three Jill Hughes, the wife of the Welsh football manager, Mark Hughes, she would have found it very difficult to be a Spice Girl and a Spice Mum. She is the type of individual who always needs someone around helping her in order to cope with daily life. Lacking confidence in her own abilities, she tends to rely on others. Her reliance on her mother, mother-in-law, younger sister and husband has led inevitably to tensions and difficulties. She admits that she is a domestic disaster, unable to switch on the washing machine or work the cooker. When she has tried her hand at washing, expensive clothes end up shrunk, discoloured or worse. These days David and Victoria send everything to the local dry cleaners and it's not hard to imagine the size of the bills.

For a woman who likes to be in control she is a notoriously untidy individual. 'Messiness must be my most annoying habit,' she says, admitting that her behaviour causes friction between David and herself. By contrast David, as self-reliant as he is self-possessed, takes on the duties of house-husband, always ready to attend to Brooklyn so that Victoria can have a lie-in. For a long time the couple didn't employ a cleaner so it was left to David to do the washing, ironing or vacuuming around their apartment in Alderley Edge. He does the cooking, usually straightforward fare like spaghetti bolognaise or lasagne, and when he isn't there, his mother comes to help out. There is a sense that without her army of surrogate mothers, Victoria would find it hard to cope with her son on her own, a little girl lost in a grown-up world. As commentator Allison Pearson noted: 'Have you noticed how it is nearly always Dad we see carrying Brooklyn and not Mum.'

These remarks were made when debate about Victoria, her weight and the difficulties of being a new mother were at their height. It was noted that she seemed lost, unsure of her place and her role in life, flailing around to find direction and meaning.

It is the conflict between the mental image she carries of being a strong positive role model for youngsters and her psychological anxieties that is most revealing. Even her bold statement: 'I think I'm a pretty positive role model for kids. I'm not out getting pissed every night, shagging loads of different men, and if they slag me off at the end of the day I don't really give a shit', which she made to startled writer Stuart Jeffries, contains the rather hysterical and depressingly vulgar defiance that is her trademark.

This is the same woman who has spoken repeatedly and rather prissily about teaching her children the value of good manners and good behaviour. Presumably this doesn't extend to polite language.

It is however the constant contrast between her seemingly defiant public attitude and pronouncements that help us understand the vulnerable uncertain woman inside the brassy public figure. The debate about her weight in the winter of 1999 revealed much about her character, as well as the impact of fame on her young and still-maturing character.

In December 1999 when she arrived for a 37th birthday lunch at the Ivy restaurant hosted by Elton John for his partner David Furnish, wearing an off-the-shoulder red leather mini dress, the change in her figure was unmistakeable.

On that chilly winter's day when other guests like Elizabeth Hurley and Helena Bonham Carter had wrapped up well, the five-foot-six-inch singer who weighed just seven and a half stone seemed to want to flaunt her jutting collarbone and stick-like legs. In a nation where an estimated 1.5 million people, overwhelmingly women, suffer from some kind of eating disorder and where the Government has opened a discussion about how the mass media, particularly women's magazines, encourage women to be dissatisfied with their size and shape, Posh Spice's problems struck a chord.

A few weeks later, in February 2000, she was keen to expose herself again, this time for London Fashion Week where Victoria, who is a size 6, wore a pair of hot pants and an evening dress slashed to the thigh. While she admitted that she was 'so petrified that she could hardly speak' she went ahead with her catwalk routine. Indeed she was so keen to parade her body that when her friend, designer Maria Grachvogel was making the outfits she insisted on showing as much flesh as possible. 'We discuss the designs for the clothes she makes for me. She says: "Let's put the split to the knee" and I always say "No, make it higher – thigh high."'

On the same day that the *Daily Mail* advised its readers on how to 'lose a stone in a flash', they observed with horror Victoria's new shape. Under the headline: 'Skeletal Spice' the paper asked the burning question of the day: 'Should she be a role model for teenage girls prone to anorexia?' It was a further episode in the national sport of celebrity weight-watching. Victoria joined a long line of other women stars, notably *Friends* favourites Courteney Cox Arquette and Jennifer Aniston, *Ally McBeal*'s Calista Flockhart and actress Elizabeth Hurley, whose lives under the spotlight had impelled them to become, according to one critic, 'like some dreadful mockery of famine victims.'

It seems that those trying to climb Mount Celebrity share a similar mindset, that control of their bodies equates to control of their lives and hence their fame. As commentator Shane Watson argued: 'Vulnerable squashy bodies belong to vulnerable weak people. An obsessive attitude to physical perfection is now the mark of the seriously ambitious.'

That she now joins these other celebrity women who are noticed as much for their physiques as their talent is rather a pity. When asked once what she meant by Girl Power she answered: 'We're saying you don't have to be skinny and six foot tall and have no spots and be beautiful 'cos we're not like that. We're normal shaped girls.'

Understandably Victoria, ever conscious of her image, was hurt by the furore not just for herself but for her mother. As she said: 'I could have a nervous breakdown. This is also saying that my mum hasn't brought me up right. It's saying that I've got a problem and no one has recognized it and no one is offering me any help. My mum is really upset about this.'

She argued that her own mother had lost three stone after giving birth to her brother Christian, that her husband David was perfectly happy with her new shape, that she ate healthily and that bringing up baby Brooklyn was such hard work that she was always on the go. 'It's irresponsible to say I'm anorexic. After a baby you are dashing about all day. I never sit down,' she said when the issue first arose, adding that she had a responsibility as a role model to young fans who could get the wrong idea. 'I'm not anorexic, I'm not bulimic and I'm not a skeleton. I'm seven and a half stone, very fit and I feel great,' she retorted on the front page of the *Daily Mirror*.

Her mother Jackie also waded in, phoning an afternoon TV show to assure viewers that her daughter was perfectly healthy. 'Victoria is working very hard and she's looking after a baby,' she argued, omitting to mention that with her busy schedule it was often her small army of surrogate parents who helped with Brooklyn.

Once again, in the life of Victoria Beckham, there is a difference between what she states defiantly in public and what goes on when the microphones are switched off and the notepads put away. She subsequently admitted that she was so worried that she went to see a family doctor to discuss her condition. He told her that she was between 14 and 21 pounds underweight for her height and frame. 'It did worry me. I did go to the doctors because I started to get paranoid,' she confessed to TV's Michael Parkinson. Far from her family being untroubled by her figure, there were reports of rows between her and David over her eating habits, while her mother was said to have urged her to have a full check-up.

Again her claims that she eats a normal healthy diet do not bear close scrutiny. At first glance her diet is a dietician's dream. She eschews fatty foods and is careful about what she eats and drinks. A typical day's menu would be fat-free Sugar Puffs in the morning, fat-free chicken tikka and plain salad for lunch, or fat-free tuna, prawns or swordfish and plain steamed vegetables in the evening. She never eats chocolate or other sweets, bingeing on fat-free crisps instead, munching through five bags in a day.

It is a virtually fat-free, high protein, low carbohydrate diet, a daily regime to which she rigidly adheres. She exercises the same self-discipline and rigour about what she eats as she did during her pursuit of fame. Although her menus seem healthy they may be lacking in essential nutrients, a deficiency of which could cause mood swings. Psychiatrist Dr Glenn Wilson observes that in a semi-starved state, levels of the brain chemical, serotonin, will be reduced and this in turn leads to depression and even suicidal states.

It is diet as a state of mind. For as far as the slender, feather-light Victoria is concerned, appearances really do matter. For her, it is not just diet but the whole package that must be groomed and immaculate, a vision of perfection. 'Do I look fat in this?' is her constant refrain when she is trying on clothes. Control is the key to understanding Victoria. While she tries as best she can to control circumstances, be it the media, her image or her career, life is an unruly beast. What she can control is her body, whether it be her looks, her weight or her shape.

In the months following Brooklyn's birth, Victoria, unhappy with her body shape and with the encouragement of her parents, went for an operation at the private Wellington Hospital in September 1999, checking in for the night under a false name. Afterwards she flew to Elton John's villa in the south of France to recuperate.

While she has long been self-conscious about the modest size of her bust – she admitted that on an appearance on the TV show *Top of the Pops* she used silicone 'falsies' – she later denied that she had had a boob job. She told Michael Parkinson: 'I haven't had a boob job. If I'd had a boob job I'd have had them done bigger than this.' Her official spokesman was less certain, saying that he could not deny that she had spent £10,000 enhancing her slim figure. Once again commentators scoffed at her claims: 'I'm afraid Mother Nature really doesn't do acorn shoulders and melon breasts on the same torso.'

By any standards 1999–2000 has been a traumatic period in her life. A new husband, a new baby and a new home to furnish and design would tax most people. Added to that are the stresses and strains of searching for a new career, a new public identity under constant public scrutiny. Most significantly she suffered her greatest weight loss during this period when she was trying to adapt to her changing role as a new mum.

Eating disorders specialist Dr Paul Flowers, a consultant psychiatrist, believes that her behaviour fits a familiar condition that he has seen many times during his career. Dr Flowers, who has treated numerous celebrities for eating disorders, has observed that their public greed for publicity and recognition, their desperation to be the centre of attention, hides a deep psychological hunger.

He says: 'They show all the signs of suffering from an eating disorder. These eating habits are phobic and extremely unhealthy. When you are losing weight it is because you are quite disturbed and depressed. After all half the time you are in a state of complete starvation, but the hunger they have is as much psychological as physical. While many people are predisposed towards anorexia it takes determination and discipline, qualities which she has in abundance, to succeed.'

It is no coincidence that many anorexics are adolescents precisely because the illness is about avoiding issues of conflict and separation with parents and others. In short it's about growing up or rather not wanting to grow up. Now in her mid-twenties, Victoria remains something of a Peter Pan figure, not yet secure in her own identity and not quite free of parental influence. The birth of Brooklyn has perhaps unconsciously forced her to address those unresolved issues in her life. Hence the potential onset of anorexia at this time.

As Dr Flowers remarks: 'She is a needy and narcissistic individual who sees the baby in terms of herself, as a fashion accessory. But the child makes great demands of a carer and for Victoria it has been a turning point in her life that has put her in touch with her own neediness. So becoming a parent is a form of role reversal. "What about me?" is her cry. She wants to be the baby in the family, to be looked after and cared for.'

At the same time the Peter Pan syndrome produces an internal conflict, wanting to grow up but being terrified of doing so. By losing weight, he argues, a troubled young woman like Victoria is trying to expel the womanly, maternal side of her. Anorexia is often linked to the cessation of regular periods.

She must be able to rationalize her distorted body shape as well, believing that it makes her look good and distinctive. Hence Victoria's need to show herself off in public, be it at Elton John's lunchtime bash or on the catwalk during London Fashion Week. 'As an anorexic, you love the attention your condition has generated,' Dr Flowers observed.

Perhaps all the attention also acted as a wake-up call for her and her family. The advice from her doctor and the disapproval of the media may have helped resolve some of her internal emotional tensions. In summer 2000, after a week's break in the South of France, she returned looking much more relaxed and womanly, sparking gossip that she may be expecting her second child. It wouldn't come as a surprise as she has frequently talked about adding three more babies to join Brooklyn. 'We've bought a huge house and I want to fill it with children,' she has said. Over the last year Victoria has learnt a lot about the reality of motherhood and as Brooklyn has grown and developed more of a personality, she seems to be where she has always wanted to be – back in control.

Certainly the completion of her new house in Sawbridge-worth, which she is scheduled to move into at the end of the year, cannot come soon enough. It will give her a base that is independent of her parents yet close enough for help when needed. Her first attempt at breaking free was something of a disaster. It seems that she never felt comfortable in their penthouse apartment in Alderley Edge, reportedly never making the effort to get to know her neighbours in the communal Victorian house, ignoring them if greeted and never attending meetings to discuss joint problems, impervious to complaint or criticism. 'They seem superior and they're not here most of the time,' one local complained.

Their neighbours became increasingly irritated by fans who hung around the gates and the fan mail that cluttered communal areas. Their two Rottweiler pets, Puffy and Snoop lived in a makeshift kennel behind the communal garages which became an unsightly and unpleasant mess. They have now been moved to the new house.

Matters came to a head in summer 2000 when one neighbour, Cybil Davis-Brummell, a former aide to Princess Alexandra, reportedly took the trouble to start a petition to ask them to leave. She complained that she had been stopped from using the communal gardens by the Beckham's minders so that Brooklyn could play there in safety.

Nor was she said to have been happy with Victoria's foul language during a dispute with a neighbour over car parking. 'Posh is really common. You can tell that when she opens her mouth,' she was quoted as saying, a comment that had academics musing how old money had always looked down on new money.

The Beckhams decided to move out, blaming snooty neighbours and nosey visitors. For all the bickering, at the heart of the matter was that issue of control again. The Queen of Herts, so used to immediate obedience to her wishes and whims, was for once not fully in control of her northern outpost.

By retreating to their southern redoubt, Victoria and David are now rulers of all they survey. They have reinforced the £2.5 million seven-bedroomed mansion in Hertfordshire set in 24 acres of grounds so that it is now secure against any assault from the outside world. Not only is the house only approachable by a private road, but they have spent £300,000 installing a high-tech security system to turn the mansion into a fortress.

They are safe in their Never Never land, able to indulge all their fantasies. Victoria is mistress of the manor, controlling the design and decoration throughout. Everywhere that is except David's snooker room which he aims to make a shrine to sport, exhibiting not just his soccer memorabilia but his collection of other sporting artefacts.

For a time they genuinely considered the idea of changing the house name from Rowneybury to Beckingham Palace. Like true royalty, David didn't care about mockery in the media. Victoria was not so sure. In the end wiser counsels prevailed.

Even for new royalty it was a dream too far.

Seven

Diary of a Long-Distance Lover

O N a crisp late-September day in the early stages of the 1999–2000 season, David Beckham arrived at The Cliff – the former racecourse turned practice pitch, graced by generations of Manchester United's greats – for the midweek training session.

The routine changes little: a light work-out to warm up; banter with his friends and team-mates, Ryan Giggs and Gary Neville; five-a-sides; practice of his speciality dead-ball kicks, and perhaps a short team talk from his manager Sir Alex Ferguson.

On this particular day the Premier League champions were no doubt gearing themselves up for the forthcoming match against long-time rivals Chelsea at Stamford Bridge on the first Sunday of October 1999. Unfortunately for United, they were to suffer their heaviest defeat of the season against the London side, losing 5-0, which was also their worst result since 1996. Beckham was substituted midway through the second half, and his lacklustre performance did not go unnoticed. 'Beckham looked like he was sulking, well and truly cheesed off that football is interfering with his social life,' noted the *Daily Mirror*.

His indifferent showing on the pitch against Chelsea that day may be partly explained by his hectic social life, but also by the strains in his domestic routine. Following the training session before the big game, he had a shower and drove from The Cliff in Salford to his £300,000 apartment in leafy Alderley Edge, the Cheshire town that is home to many of Manchester's so-called glitterati, including other United players such as Jaap Stam,

DIARY OF A LONG-DISTANCE LOVER

Dwight Yorke and Andy Cole. Unlike his team-mates, Beckham rarely lingers at the training ground. More often than not he leaves before the communal lunch that Sir Alex Ferguson encourages in order to build team spirit, bound for home to see his wife and child instead.

En route to Alderley Edge he is a familiar face both at the McDonalds hamburger restaurant – where he holds a gold card – and at his local fish and chip shop. In an era when English professional footballers are encouraged to follow Continental habits and eat a wholesome, balanced diet, Beckham is an unreconstructed junk food addict. On one occasion he stopped at a motorway service station well after midnight and tucked into a full English breakfast. Indeed his daily diet of hamburgers and fries or fish and chips and takeaway food would shock progressive coaches like the Arsenal manager Arsene Wenger. The Frenchman famously weaned his team off their habits of stodgy food and drinking bouts, teaching them that if they wanted their careers to last longer in the modern game they had to respect their bodies.

On this day though Beckham knew he faced another 185-mile slog down Britain's clogged motorways before he could rejoin his wife and child. As was their routine Victoria and Brooklyn were staying with her parents at their Hertfordshire mansion. During the three-hour journey, he had plenty to think about. The man he called the 'gaffer' had just handed him a record club fine of £50,000 – the equivalent of two weeks' wages – for breaking a club curfew. His high-profile arrival, wearing a £75 silk headscarf, at designer Jade Jagger's party in Covent Garden during London Fashion Week, only hours before the team flew to Austria for an important Champions' League game against Sturm Graz, had proved the last straw for Sir Alex, and Beckham was punished for compromising the team at such a crucial time. So as he drove down the M6 he surely realized that by heading south, just prior to another important fixture, he was tempting fate – and another heavy fine – again.

If he had hoped for a relaxing evening with his wife and child when he arrived in Hertfordshire, he was to be disappointed. Victoria had agreed to join her Spice Girl friend and colleague Emma Bunton who was launching her television career by hosting the fifth anniversary celebrations of the pop music channel VH-1. So he chauffeured Victoria to the event at the Atlantis Gallery bar in London's East End, risking the attention of the inevitable posse of waiting photographers. He must have known he couldn't afford to be snapped again at such a high profile bash so soon after his last dressing down from Ferguson. It was just a question of whiling away a few anonymous hours while Victoria caroused in yet another VIP bar.

One wonders whether he thought all the trouble was worthwhile. Here was one of Britain's most talented football players, whose boots sold at auction at Christie's for £13,800, whose signed shirts sell for £7,500 apiece and whose fans have been known to rummage through dustbins outside his hairdresser's salon for locks of his golden gelled hair, reduced to skulking around London like a man on the run.

After a couple of hours he returned to the venue, where he was seen but not captured on camera, to pick up Victoria and her party, and drive them home. He would have had little time for rest before the next morning's training session back in Manchester. A snatched night's sleep and a 370-mile round trip – hardly the best training for a professional athlete upon whose slim shoulders rest the hopes and ambitions not only of Manchester United supporters but millions of England fans.

After the £50,000 fine, the gruelling post-training drive to and from Hertfordshire, and his team's biggest defeat since 1996, it had been a bad week for the man voted most stylish man of the year by readers of the men's magazine *GQ*, and most valuable player in the Champions' League – two awards that characterized the conflict between his professional life and public image.

The endless commute from Manchester to Goff's Oak or London is a regular and tiring routine, an unsettled pattern of life that reflects the irreconcilable demands of two of the most important people in his life: his wife and his manager. The battle for the heart and mind of David Beckham is more than just a fight between two stubborn, determined and strong-willed individuals; it is a clash of culture and generations.

Born in Glasgow during the war years, Alex Ferguson's self-control, discipline and will to win have made him the outstanding football manager of his era. A life-long Labour Party supporter, he is a man who values hard work, loyalty and commitment. Indeed, in his autobiography, tellingly entitled *Managing My Life*, he singled out Beckham for his diligence: 'David Beckham is Britain's finest striker of a football not because of God-given talent but because he practises with a relentless application that the vast majority of less gifted players wouldn't contemplate.'

For Ferguson football comes first, middle and last. He has no time for distractions, particularly drinking and partying, and woe betide the player who stretches his patience or resists his strict regime. As numerous idols of the terraces have found to their cost, it is a quick route to the transfer market. Stories of him throwing soft drinks at recalcitrant players are, by his own admission, only a slight exaggeration. Yet Beckham acknowledges: 'There's not one player at United who doesn't have some kind of fear of the gaffer, but it's not dread of him, more a respect for what he stands for. And what he's done for us all.' Even before Victoria came on the scene, David, like most of the team, had suffered the 'hairdryer treatment', enduring a close-range verbal blast from the manager.

At the same time, over the last few years, the rise of player power (particularly resulting from the Bosman ruling which enables an out-of-contract footballer to move clubs on a free transfer if demands for a more generous contract are not met), and the influence of agents and advisers as well as increased player sponsorship have forced Ferguson to modify his steely approach. As Ferguson's biographer, sports writer Harry Harris says: 'Managers like Alex Ferguson are a dying breed, men used to ruling by fear. He is a dictatorial manager whose power has diminished over the years. He demands a high level of fitness and dedication from his players and knows from experience that they go downhill rapidly if they are out on the tiles all night.'

Rock and roll it certainly isn't. As far as Ferguson is concerned, in the male-dominated world of professional football, the role of a player's wife is simple: to ensure a well-ordered and preferably quiet home life so that the player puts on his finest performance on, rather than off, the pitch. Enter into this equation a multi-millionairess who is both more famous and richer than her player partner; a powerful, ambitious woman used to the trappings of success and the glamorous lifestyle of a pop superstar.

Victoria Beckham is the epitome of the Me First generation of the 1980s, combining the self-centred acquisitiveness of the Thatcher years with a highly attuned sense of what is right for her and what is hers by right. She is a modern woman who is not intimidated by men, a pop icon ruthlessly determined to achieve further success for herself and her husband, and at the same time she is wholly unconcerned about and unaware of the tribal loyalties and passions aroused by football in either her husband, his manager or their fans.

Her complete lack of interest in the sport can be summed up by a remark she made after David had scored a sublime goal from a dead-ball kick. She had dutifully watched his performance on television and when he phoned her after the game she congratulated him, but added: 'Your roots really need doing.' On another occasion in May 2000 after he had scored his fiftieth goal for Manchester United, Victoria genuinely thought it was his fiftieth goal that season. It was a blunder that only endeared her to him all the more.

From the moment Alex Ferguson told David to stop his endless chatter with Victoria on his mobile phone during the team's coach journey to a 1997 European Cup semi-final meeting with Borussia Dortmund in Germany, conflict has never been far away. It has been a source of sadness for Ferguson to watch the changes in the young man whose career he carefully nurtured when he first came to Manchester as a promising teenager more than eleven years ago. As Ferguson says: 'Gone is the fun-loving lad of a few years ago and in his place is a seriously private person, with inner reaches that few can penetrate.'

David's own self-belief was bolstered by the unceasing support of his parents, Ted and Sandra, particularly his father although there is the sense too that David was the vessel for Ted's thwarted ambition. An enthusiastic amateur footballer in his youth, he shared with his young son his great passion for the game, his patient coaching skills and the unlikely dedication of a North London lad to Manchester United.

When he was sixteen it was no surprise that David chose to sign for Manchester United as an apprentice and moved on from collecting glasses from punters at Walthamstow Greyhound Track to a far more prosperous career away from family and friends. Even though he moved into digs in Manchester he and his parents remained just as close, although Ted and Sandra must have clocked up thousands of motorway miles to support their son and his dream – a footballing prodigy straight out of the pages of a schoolboy comic book. His happiness and enthusiasm can be seen in pictures of the young apprentice. The brooding surliness and the grim-faced me-against-the-world hostility were for the future.

As David settled into the strict Old Trafford regime comparisons with the legendary George Best were inevitable. Here was that same explosive mix of outstanding natural talent and undeniable glamour on and off the field.

Manager Alex Ferguson was wise to keep David's feet firmly on the ground by sending him for a month on loan to Third Division Preston North End. As Beckham admitted, the four-week stay boosted his game immeasurably: 'I needed to be picked up a little bit, to be encouraged, and Preston did that for me.'

It should also have reminded him that his life and future in the game were dictated by the whim of one man – the gaffer.

In less than five years as a first-team regular, Beckham has become one of the most successful players in British football history. He has winner's medals from four Premier League titles, two FA Cups and one Champions' League victory. He was the 1997 PFA Young Player of the Year, came second in the FIFA World Player of the Year in 1999, and is an automatic choice to pull on an England shirt.

And yet along with the sweet taste of success has come the sourness and vitriol that only an idol who has fallen from grace can truly savour. Beckham has drunk from this cup in full measure during his short career. The routine jeers and taunts he suffered solely as a Manchester United player were nothing compared to what he experienced once he started dating Posh Spice. Chants about her preferred sexual position were and are commonplace. Sometimes the fans' relentless antagonism has the desired effect and leads to him making rash challenges and petulant fouls; other times the abuse simply makes him play better.

A moment of madness during the World Cup in June 1998 sealed his fate as an object of hatred and derision. Much had been expected of Beckham during the build-up to the tournament and there was surprise bordering on astonishment when the England coach Glenn Hoddle dropped him from the team, arguing that he did not feel the national playmaker was 'focused enough' for the opening match against Tunisia. A question of temperament exacerbated by David's celebrity lifestyle had given Hoddle pause for thought.

His club manager Alex Ferguson had been equally worried ever since his star player first started seeing Victoria Adams. A besotted Beckham had regularly flown from Manchester to Ireland to spend time with his girlfriend during her year as a tax exile. Not surprisingly this did not fit in with his manager's ideas of focus and fitness. However Ferguson took issue with Hoddle when the latter forced the young man to face a media conference to discuss his decision to leave him out of the team, calling it 'an example of bad human relations'. David answered the hail of public criticism in the most effective way known to him, by proving his brilliance on the pitch. In the second game against Romania, he came on as substitute to replace the injured Paul Ince, and making his presence felt, linked up with Alan Shearer to help set up Michael Owen's equalizing goal. Despite his efforts, a late winner from Romania led to a 2-1 defeat for the England team. Against Colombia, however, the result was very different. From a free kick outside the Colombian penalty area, he scored a scintillating goal to give England a 2-0 lead that they clung to until the final whistle.

Within days his triumph turned to disaster in a match against Argentina when he became only the second England player to be sent off in a World Cup tournament. During a match in which England had the upper hand, the Argentinian midfield player Diego Simeone scythed Beckham down. As Beckham lay poleaxed, Simeone bent down and gave his hair a tug. The red mist took over; Beckham flicked him with his foot, a petulant gesture that had Danish referee Kim Nielsen reaching for the red card. When the remaining ten-man English team eventually lost the match on penalties, David Beckham's moment of madness was widely regarded as the main cause of the national side's defeat.

As his club manager noted he could not have been more vilified if he had committed murder or high treason. Fans ignored Glenn Hoddle's plea that Beckham should not be made the scapegoat for England's premature exit from the World Cup. An effigy of him was hung and burnt outside one pub, West Ham fans planned a mass showing of red cards to the luckless international at their next game against Manchester United, while the nation's football pundits had a field day analysing his shortcomings. When he returned for training at Old Trafford he needed police protection.

It is an experience seared into his soul, one that he acknowledges he will never be allowed to forget. He was hounded with a cruel intensity that would have broken lesser men but Beckham drew his strength from Victoria, flying to join her in New York where she was touring with the Spice Girls. 'I just hope I handled it with dignity. It's certainly made me mature a lot as a person and a player,' he has said, admitting that he does not find it easy to discuss his innermost feelings in public.

After another season of abuse and praise, the love-hate relationship he experienced with the fans reached its climax during the Euro 2000 competition in Belgium; after a match against Portugal he gave an obscene one-fingered gesture to England supporters who taunted him about his family, shouting that his wife was a whore and hoping his son Brooklyn died of cancer.

Labour peer Lord Hattersley complained that Beckham was a 'national liability' because he reacted like a man who had no control over his emotions. 'You don't beat yobbishness by being a yob,' he opined. In contrast though the overwhelming majority of commentators and fans had sympathy for his plight. As the present England coach Kevin Keegan said: 'It is nothing

Right: At the wedding of David's friend and team-mate Philip Neville in December 1999. Although female guests were asked to dress in the Manchester United colours of red, black and white, Victoria stole the limelight, wearing a strapless, coffee-coloured dress split revealingly to the thigh.

Above: David reclines on the practice pitch, revealing the tattoo of his son's name, Brooklyn, inscribed at the base of his spine. Concealed beneath his shirt is a guardian angel tattoo he had etched between his shoulder blades. 'Brooklyn is beneath so it's like he's watching over him,' David explained.

Far right: David had his son's name emblazoned on a special seat in the rear of his hand-built TVR sports car. Brooklyn's name is also printed on his father's golf shoes (below).

bove: May 6 2000: On the day that
Manchester United receive the Premier
League Championship trophy. Victoria and
Brooklyn (kitted out by his father in a replica
shirt) join David on the pitch to share in the
celebrations.

Right: Designer baby: Victoria and Brooklyn
out shopping together.

Above: David's parents, Ted and Sandra Beckham, who have supported their son throughout his illustrious career.

Below: David attends his sister Lynne's wedding in Hornchurch, Essex, in October 1999. He is pictured with the groom Colin Every, Lynne and their younger sister Joanne.

ght: David, alone at Lynne's wedding. he Beckhams were disappointed that ctoria and Brooklyn did not attend.

elow: The Adams family arriving at e Brit Awards, Earls Court. Left to ght, Victoria's brother Christian and s girlfriend Lucy, Victoria's younger ster Louise, and her parents, Jackie d Tony.

Above: Public Enemy Number One: David receives a red card playing for England against Argentina in the 1998 World Cup, after kicking out at Diego Simeone, following a reckless challenge by the Argentinian.

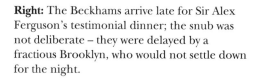

Right: The Beckhams arrive late for Sir Alex Ferguson's testimonial dinner; the snub was not deliberate – they were delayed by a fractious Brooklyn, who would not settle down for the night.

Above: David attends the Prince's Trust Anniversary dinner at the Opera House, Manchester, accompanied by his team-mates and friends Ryan Giggs, and Phil Neville.

Above right: David hit the headlines after shaving off his trademark floppy golden hair. He is pictured with David Gardner, one of his best friends.

Right: Caught on camera: Victoria videos the triumphant day at Old Trafford on 6 May 2000, when Manchester United received the Premier League Championship trophy.

David has an insatiable appetite for fast sports cars, each bearing a number plate incorporating the number 7 and initials DVB. David's ever-increasing collection of cars include a Porsche Carrera, an XKR Jaguar, an Aston Martin and a Mercedes convertible.

Above: David leaves Stockport Magistrates Court accompanied by bodyguard Mark Niblett (left) and Ned Kelly, head of security at Manchester United, on 9 December 1999, following a hearing for a speeding violation. He was fined £800 and banned for eight months, but on appeal at Minshul Crown Court a week later, a sympathetic judge revoked the ban.

Below: Victoria and David attend the controversial Mike Tyson v Julius Francis fight at the M.E.N. Arena in Manchester, in January 2000 – they were booed and jeered when their presence was announced to the crowd.

Left: A slim-line, 'size 6' Victoria takes to the catwalk in February 2000 for London Fashion Week, freely admitting that she was 'so petrified that she could hardly speak'. Her featherlight physique post-childbirth has been under the constant scrutiny of the press, and suspicions that she battles with an eating disorder are rife.

Despite the difference in her appearance before (above and below) and after childbirth, Victoria has asserted 'I'm not anorexic, I'm not bulimic and I'm not a skeleton'.

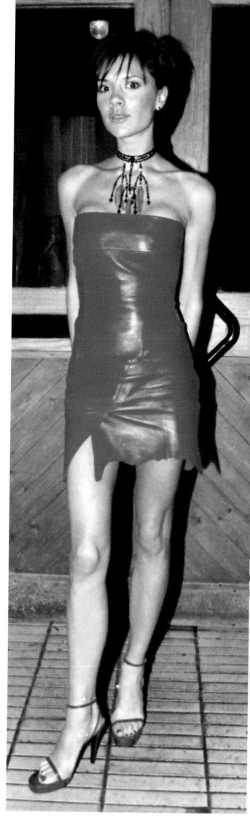

Out in style: Undaunted by the critics, Victoria shows off her slim physique.

Right: At the Art of Barbie Ball in December 1999, Victoria wears a pink Barbie dress and poses between Elton John and his partner David Furnish. David Beckham surprised his wife when he turned up in a hastily-made suit matching the style of Barbie's boyfriend Ken.

Below: The four remaining Spice Girls wow the audience at the start of their Christmas concerts in early December at the Manchester Arena.

Below: The Spice Girls are overcome with emotion at the Brit Awards held at Earls Court in March 2000, following a poignant performance of 'Goodbye' and the receipt of a special award for their outstanding contribution to pop music. Victoria was particularly on edge throughout the day.

above: Prior to the release of her first solo single, Victoria performs 'Out Of Your Mind' with True Steppers and Dane Bowers at the Party in the Park concert in Hyde Park on 9 July 2000. There was criticism that she had mimed the hit single.

above right: During a rigorous campaign to promote her first solo single, Victoria is pictured at the G.A.Y. event at London's Astoria on 5 August 2000.

right: Victoria's promotional gigs continue the following day at the Radio One Roadshow in Middlesbrough.

David accompanied Victoria on a whistlestop tour of Britain to promote her first solo single. In Oldham an estimated 6,000 fans wanted to catch a glimpse of the celebrity couple. Victoria's efforts were in vain. She was pipped to the top spot in the singles chart by Spiller.

to do with the game of football. It is something we all have to put up with at times and we do it quite well, but there is a point where every human reaches a limit and it has gone well beyond that. I can't understand why it happens.'

If Keegan had no obvious explanation for the fans' behaviour, journalist Julie Burchill ascribed it to the homo-erotic relationship between fans and their idols. 'Physical rather than cerebral, thoughtful rather than articulate, Beckham is not a neurotic career-obsessed salary man, but one who has his priorities completely sorted out at an impressively early age. Not a lad, but a real man. And it is for this – not for losing football matches – that so many of the inadequates currently rallying round the England flag hate him.' Others were not so sure, arguing that the fans were angered by Beckham because he was allowing his wife to distract him from his job and dilute his prodigious talent. Maybe it is precisely because his priorities are not nearly so settled as Burchill assumes that he has encountered so many problems both on and off the football pitch.

Observers had not been slow to notice the conflicting pressures on David, which seemingly contributed to outbreaks of petulance on the pitch during the 1999-2000 season. During the Sturm Graz game he was lucky not to be sent off. He was given a red card for a vicious challenge during the World Club Championships in Brazil in January 2000. At Anfield he was involved in an ugly stamping incident with Liverpool skipper Jamie Redknapp. There were also allegations that he made obscene gestures to the crowd at Elland Road where Leeds United supporters were baiting him about his wife. Such was the concern that Graham Bean, the compliance officer for the Football Association, wanted to meet him to discuss his disciplinary record. In mitigation David has had many things on his mind. He worries about his wife and child dreadfully: 'I'm thinking all the time about my little boy and Victoria. All the time, every minute.' Concerns not just about their general well-being, but also their safety. The death threats, abusive letters and security concerns have naturally played on the mind of the young man, drawing him ever more tightly into a close circle of family and friends.

Having had numerous close encounters with referees for bouts of unacceptable behaviour during that season, a question mark still hangs over his professional temperament, but in everyday life too others have noticed the changes in his demeanour; the watchful eyes, a constant wariness in his gait in readiness for paparazzi ambushes, and a face contorted with anger often replaces the once cheeky grin.

Furthermore the famous short fuse on the pitch is now in evidence away from the terraces. Often when he is driving he will become very aggressive with those he considers to have 'cut him up' on the road. Even autograph hunters have caught the rough edge of his tongue. Normally he is very considerate with fans, having asserted: 'I don't like bad manners, I never have done, which is why I never refuse autographs,' but persistent autograph hunters known as 'giffers' get short shrift. On one occasion when a Liverpool youngster asked for his signature, the boy received a torrent of abuse. 'He is so unpleasant and rude that I wouldn't bother asking him again,' said the youngster. 'David and Victoria upset a lot of people with their attitude.'

Photographers who have been snapping him since he arrived as a raw teenage talent are now regular targets for abuse. When one cameraman took a picture of the Beckhams leaving the children's store Daisy and Tom in central Manchester, David's reaction was instantly aggressive. He ran across the road and threatened to stab the photographer if he took another picture.

Beckham is certainly not the first celebrity to have clashed with cameramen. It is part of the psychology of stardom. As the comedian Fred Allen observes, a celebrity is 'a person who strives to become well known, then wears dark glasses in order to avoid being recognized.'

There is though a deeper malaise, his anger expressing an internal tension that is gnawing away at his love of football and threatening to undermine his tremendous talent. For all his medals and trophies, all the adulation and acclaim, David Beckham leads an unsettled life, a long distance commuter with no fixed abode and a suitcase his constant companion.

The orbit of his world has shifted its axis and naturally his parents constantly worry that his changing priorities will affect his professional game. Over the years they have built up a friendly relationship of mutual respect with Sir Alex Ferguson. They appreciate the chances he has given their son, well aware of his firm belief in loyalty to the team and to the club's code of discipline. As they see David drawn into the circles of showbiz and celebrity, his glamorous lifestyle inevitably preys on their minds, especially as he has marital connections to a family with no links or interest in the game. David himself has said: 'Football's not the only thing in my life any more. Things that were important before just don't seem as important now that I have Brooklyn and Victoria.'

His parents are not the only ones to be concerned. The effect of Victoria on a national footballing asset has sparked a countrywide debate. There have been public accusations that she hated Manchester, wanting him to leave Old Trafford for a southern club or one in Europe, and that her relationship with Sir Alex was less than cordial. While she has made no secret about her lack of interest in football, she has publicly denied these stories, saying they were 'hurtful and unfair'. 'I know how much it means for David to play for United, so I'd never put him in a position like that,' she said, emphasizing that she was happy living in Manchester. At the time observers saw her utterances as an attempt to be tactful. As Harry Harris says:

'Behind the scenes Victoria would prefer to live in London. The reality is that she doesn't like Manchester although she has been very diplomatic about it.'

In *Forever Spice*, however, she refers to earlier tension between David and herself over his desire to play for Manchester United. 'We had a bit of a dispute on the phone because he is re-signing his contract in Manchester. I was a bit hurt because I was hoping deep down he would sign for a London club.' More recently Victoria has conceded, 'I'd be lying if I said we're going to be here for ever and ever. Footballers move abroad at some stage in their career so I'm sure we will.'

Victoria is constantly thinking of ways to enable David to spend more time in the south with her and her family. The manager ruled out suggestions that Beckham was allowed to commute by helicopter as too dangerous, rejecting also a scheme to convert a camper van so that David could sleep as a chauffeur drove him on the motorway. Even though Stansted airport is only half an hour's drive from Goff's Oak, he dare not travel south by air, as word would soon get back to the 'gaffer'.

The burgeoning conflict between his professional and personal life was perfectly illustrated at Christmas 1999. The couple argued over her desire to spend the festive season with her family in Hertfordshire even though he had an important league game at home against Bradford City on Boxing Day. The bickering went on for several days and, as is usually the case, Victoria prevailed. So on Christmas Eve, while Victoria appeared on a TV show, David drove down to Goff's Oak after training. He stayed at the Adamses' on Christmas Day, driving north late in the evening for the match a few hours later.

So David is left with the worst of all worlds, shuttling up and down the motorway at all hours of the day and night, snatching a few precious hours with his son and wife before returning to training or a game. It is a lifestyle that would even surprise Ferguson, who noted in his autobiography that he had spoken to David during his courting days about the number of flights he was making to Ireland to see Victoria. 'I had to stress that he had obligations to his own talent and to his team-mates. Fortunately, that is no longer a concern. Now that Victoria and David have settled in Cheshire with their baby son Brooklyn, normal habits have resumed.'

In reality David's life as a long-distance commuter has continued, the footballer regularly leaving her parents' home at dawn for the long drive back to Manchester. Nor is this a temporary state of affairs. The couple's decision to buy a luxury mansion in the Hertfordshire village of Sawbridgeworth (seventeen miles from Goff's Oak), so that Victoria can be near her parents, has condemned David to this gruelling routine for the foreseeable future. David himself has denied that he commutes frequently between London and Manchester. 'If I was travelling up from London at six every morning, I think the strain would start to tell.'

It is not just a question of distance, or her jealousy when he is away or her closeness to her family, but her sharp commercial attitude that seems to have further unsettled her husband. Doubtless she feels that as David is such a gifted player and a valuable asset to the club then he deserves special treatment. This runs counter to the ethos that runs through Alex Ferguson's blood, that loyalty, team spirit and discipline are vital qualities for a football player. The world has moved on. So for example David's advisers argue that he is entitled to a share of Manchester United's merchandise, as it is his name on the shirts and other memorabilia the club are happy to sell and profit from.

Indeed, for all the criticism she has attracted, Victoria Beckham has a shrewd commercial head and an eye for the main chance. These are the priorities that inform her thinking about his career. She is acutely aware that fame is ephemeral and that they both only have a few years to exploit their earnings potential. At a time when sport is big business, she knows instinctively that loyalty comes a poor second to money. Unlike celebrities of yesterday who frittered away their talents or money and ended up with nothing, Victoria is one of a new breed of stars who want to control and merchandise every facet of their lives.

It irked her when United team captain Roy Keane landed a new contract worth £52,000 a week. Immediately she started agitating for her husband to negotiate a pay rise, publicly voicing her concerns during a radio interview when she pleaded for a new deal.

As far as Victoria is concerned football is a commodity and she believes that her husband should exploit it to the full. If that means going abroad, so be it. Doubtless she has already calculated that the time spent commuting between Stansted and Milan, for example, is only marginally greater than to Manchester. Already AC Milan President Silvio Berlusconi has indicated that Beckham is on his shopping list and the astronomic sum of £50 million has been mentioned.

In a couple of years, Sir Alex is due to retire and David's contract will be up for renewal. It is possible that not only will we see the departure of the most successful manager in the modern game, but that David Beckham and other United stars may also feel it is time to move on. It will be the end of an era.

Until then though Victoria will continue to maintain an uneasy relationship with Sir Alex. Her sharp commercial sense, her domestic demands and her unwillingness, as a successful entertainer, to kow-tow to the demands of a manager and club, has been a recipe for continual conflict between two of the most influential people in David's life.

Perhaps her first direct experience of what she will have considered as unreasonable and unfair demands made of her husband by Sir Alex came during their honeymoon in July 1999. Despite the couple's pleadings, David was ordered back to Old Trafford for training, and so they were forced to abandon a ten-day trip to the Indian Ocean. Instead of sunning themselves on a faraway desert island, the newly-weds spent a few days in the south of France before flying home so that David could join his team training for the new season. On his return David found himself reduced to playing in the reserves against the part-timers, Selby Town.

If it was Ferguson's way of bringing his star player back down to earth after the glamour and glitter of his wedding in Ireland, then it did little to improve Victoria's opinion of him. A relationship euphemistically described as 'cool' went into the deep freeze when David received the £50,000 fine following the London Fashion Week incident. As Sir Alex says: 'Everybody knows that I have not always seen eye to eye with Beckham. The showbiz element in his life, made inevitable by the pop-star status of his wife, Victoria, has sometimes caused me to worry about a possible threat to his chances of giving maximum expression to his huge talent.'

By a sublime irony, the greatest cause of friction between the Beckhams and Sir Alex has been the latest addition to his family, baby Brooklyn. On the night of Ferguson's testimonial dinner in Manchester, hosted by TV interviewer Eamonn Holmes, the Beckhams arrived at 8.55 p.m. for an event due to start at 7 p.m. By the time they were seated by a stony-faced Ned Kelly, the head of Manchester United security, the event was well under way.

The snub however was not deliberate. Brooklyn would not settle down for the night and as the minutes ticked by he grew more and more agitated. As he would not respond to the babysitter's attempts to soothe him, the couple had to delay their departure until he had settled. By the time the domestic crisis was over the couple were very late for the important event, and destined for column space in next day's papers.

It was another episode involving David's concern over Brooklyn that led to his most damaging fall out with Ferguson.

On the night of Thursday 17 February 2000, Brooklyn, then eleven months old, spent a restless night at Goff's Oak, continually being sick and running a temperature. At dawn the next day it was a very worried and tired David Beckham who left his son behind to drive to Manchester to join his team-mates in training for that Sunday's top of the table clash with Leeds United. When he departed Brooklyn was still unwell and as David headed north he grew increasingly anxious about his son's condition.

After driving on the motorway for an hour or so he had got himself into such a state of anxiety that he decided to turn back and miss morning training. However when he contacted the club to inform them of his domestic problem they were probably left with the understanding that he was at home in Alderley Edge. As luck would have it Victoria was photographed with her sister Louise in Knightsbridge on a three-hour shopping spree. That morning as Brooklyn made a rapid recovery she and her mother Jackie had gone to the local Marks and Spencer.

While Brooklyn was well, David's relationship with his manager was now on the critical list. When he reported for training on Saturday morning he faced an angry and very public tongue-lashing from Ferguson who told him to sort out his priorities, that the club came before everything else. Then he unceremoniously kicked him out of the new training ground at Carrington, shouting: 'Get out of here, get off the pitch and get out now.' He was dropped for the match at Elland Road, fined £50,000, and suffered the ignominy of watching the game, boots in hand, from the sidelines. It was, crowed the *Daily Mail*, a triumph for discipline and integrity over celebrity and distraction.

For David Beckham it was a salutary experience. His parents, who had driven to Leeds to watch the match as they do for all his games, would have viewed the incident as justification of all their concerns and warnings. Unlike Victoria and her family, they knew the manager, and were only too aware of his strict attitude and his history of ditching players who get too big for their boots. A surprised Ted Beckham first heard about the bust-up in a brief phone call from David who told him he had been dropped. Seemingly anxious not to make a bad situation any worse he said, 'I don't want to upset the apple cart. Whatever has happened is between David and the club.'

David's parents will have been fearful, probably with good reason, that he was jeopardizing his glittering career at Manchester United. Afterwards Ferguson believed that his tough approach had brought the Victoria and David to their senses. He noted: 'The after-effects of the episode were entirely positive. It brought home to David the seriousness of my attitude about how he should prepare for games. Living in the south of England was not fair to me, the club, his team-mates or the fans who have supported him so loyally. Nor in football terms was it fair to him.'

For Victoria, who is well aware of the commercial possibilities in football, the incident served as a reminder that if Ferguson were provoked much more he might decide, without hesitation, to sell David to a club not of their choosing. So it is little wonder then that she regards her visits to Old Trafford as more of a duty than a pleasure, a necessary function to show loyalty to her husband.

Few can blame her for being reluctant to attend matches at Old Trafford. The vicious chants sung by the away fans against herself and Brooklyn at the ground, as well as continual death threats sent to her home, make her wary of risking too much public exposure at football games. Indeed her husband advised her not to attend the vital crunch match against Germany at Euro 2000 because he was worried about her well-being.

Safety is her main concern when she goes to Old Trafford. On arrival at the ground she is the only footballer's wife whose car is permitted to drive right up to the entrance of the stadium. When she gets out of the car, stewards make a cordon so that she and her party only have to walk a few paces before they are safely inside.

Those at the ground note that in the last season she spent little time actually watching a match, preferring to stay in the club crèche with her son. For a long time the shouts of the fans upset Brooklyn and she put cotton wool in his ears to protect him. Not that it's much better for her, the stares of fans as well as the attentions of amateur photographers make it an uncomfortable experience. After the match she waits in the players' lounge for David, rarely speaking to anyone else apart from his mother. With a couple of exceptions, she has done virtually nothing to build a rapport with players' partners or United staff. It is apparent even to casual observers that she finds the whole experience a trial.

The one occasion she seemed to enjoy was when she watched Brooklyn and his father walk on the pitch when his team were presented with the League Championship on 6 May 2000, following a 3-1 defeat of Tottenham Hotspur at the last home game of the season. David, who had organized a special kit for Brooklyn, did a lap of honour with his son, all the while watched by Victoria and their respective parents.

It did little however to change her thoughts on the beautiful game. Despite the success enjoyed by her husband, and the money to be earned in top-flight football, she has her own ideas for Brooklyn's future. 'I would definitely prefer him to be a golfer. It's a better profession than a footballer.'

Eight

Fast and Furious

EVER since he can remember, Chris Neill had wanted to be a professional photographer. He still recalls the day when Frank, his father, gave him his first camera, an Agfa worth £5, for his fourteenth birthday. 'It was a great thrill,' he says.

At the age of sixteen he left his comprehensive school in Blackley, Manchester, still dreaming of the day that his first picture would be published. For his first job he worked as a messenger on his local paper, the *Manchester Evening News*, for £35 a week, simply so that he could vicariously indulge his passion for photography. After a hard day's work he would catch a bus to his local night school, Plant Hill, where he studied the art of developing and printing pictures.

When he had a few hours spare, he wandered around the city taking photographs of anything that caught his eye. During the riots at Strangeways prison in 1990 he spent days camped outside the jail, watching prisoners throwing stones and hurling expletives, capturing the unfolding action on roll after roll of film. He was rewarded with exclusive pictures of the jail being stormed, shots that gained him his first commission from the BBC. His hard work and determination caught the eye of the Prince of Wales Trust who gave him a grant of £1,500 to set up his own photographic business.

From that moment he has never looked back, building up a modest agency to support himself, his wife and five young children, two of them from his wife's first marriage. His work is the run-of-the-mill routine of a provincial photographer:

weddings, portraits and legal work. Not for him the glamour of photoshoots for glossy magazines or for that matter the notoriety of the long-lens paparazzi. In a good year he makes £25,000 – what David Beckham earns in a week.

As a life-long Manchester United fan he naturally wanted to learn to take sports photographs. Opportunities were limited. Week after week he asked United to let him take pictures on match days, but since he was an unaccredited freelance, they refused. Instead Chris, now thirty-four, began taking straight-forward portraits of the players at Old Trafford or leaving the training ground in their expensive sports cars. The slimly-built Mancunian and his white Ford Fiesta car became a familiar feature at the United ground. He was beginning to build a modest portfolio of off-duty snaps but during the early 1990s there was little demand for his efforts. The explosion of interest in footballers as celebrity superstars, off the pitch as well as on, was just around the corner.

Enter Eric Cantona. The arrival of the mercurial Frenchman added a certain glamour and *joie de vivre* to the Manchester scene – and not a little controversy. When he was banned from playing for several months after he kung fu-kicked a Crystal Palace fan, Monsieur Cantona and Manchester United were in the news for all the wrong reasons. One afternoon Chris visited the United training ground, noticed Cantona playing in a friendly game and took a few pictures. What he did not realize at the time was that Cantona had been banned by the Football Association from playing even in casual games. Chris sold the pictures to a national newspaper for £1,000 and the result was further trouble both for Cantona and for United.

For Chris, on the other hand, it was his lucky break. 'Before I knew it, at last there was demand for my pictures,' he recalls. He paid a price, however. The club, whose 'siege mentality' towards the media is well-known, blamed the messenger – in this case the photographer – for their star player's misfortune, rather than their own underhand behaviour. A few seasons down the road Chris was to pay a heavier price still.

He was still taking photographs of the precocious crop of young players – Nicky Butt, Ryan Giggs, Gary and Phil Neville, and of course David Beckham. Usually they were friendly and co-operative and several, including Beckham, asked him to frame the portraits he took of them. Indeed on one occasion a famous United player took him to his new house and asked him to provide framed pictures of his glory days to decorate his new games room.

But as United players began to make it on to the front pages rather than the back pages there was a cooling of attitude towards Chris and another photographer, the only other free-lance cameraman who regularly photographed United players. If the arrival of Eric Cantona had ignited media interest, the romance between David Beckham and Posh Spice caused it to explode. Neither press nor public could get enough of the prince and princess of soccer and pop. As *OK!* announced in a headline when the couple were introduced to HRH the Prince of Wales: 'The King and Queen meet Prince Charles'. The irony was not intended.

The arrival of Victoria Adams, as she was then, on the Manchester United scene changed everything. While Posh Spice has made her name and fortune through her music and image, she loathes the freelance photographers who make their living taking pictures of her. In the early days of the Spice Girls, photographers remember her as friendly and amenable, eager to help a snapper to get a good shot. After her engagement to David, however, she became regular front-page news, rapidly assuming the late Princess Diana's mantle as the favourite cover girl of the tabloids. Like Diana, she was constantly hounded through the streets of London by an intimidating pack of paparazzi whose aggressive attitude makes their victims feel, as the late Princess herself once said, that they have been 'raped'.

As a result she takes a dim view of the paparazzi who dog her on an almost daily trail of retail therapy in London's ritzy Knightsbridge, tailing her from Prada to Gucci, on to Dolce and Gabbana, over to Harrods and back to Prada again. And as they sit in pavement cafés waiting for the next celebrity to walk into their web, the freelance cameramen talk in equally disparaging terms about Posh Spice, recalling the verbal and sometimes physical assaults they suffer when they dare to photograph the media's new princess. One experienced paparazzo who has followed her throughout her career says of her: 'Now she is morose and rude. It doesn't have to be like this. Other Spice Girls are still fine. Mel C for example is always co-operative. Fame doesn't seem to have changed her. Not Victoria.'

There is a frisson of fear too. The photographic agencies they supply know that Posh is their bread and butter and are reluctant to risk her displeasure. Several agencies refused to supply pictures for this book, afraid that it might upset Victoria, a woman whose influence extends deep into the heartland of tabloid journalism.

Her uncompromising attitude is not uncommon. There exists a 'celebrity syndrome' in which media stars become so used to being surrounded by yes-men and other fawning acolytes that when they come across those who treat them not as icons to be worshipped but as normal people they find it difficult to handle. Thus singer Diana Ross refused to submit to a routine security search at Heathrow airport because she did not believe that the rules which applied to ordinary travellers should also apply to her.

Dr Glenn Wilson, who has made a study of celebrity psychology, observes: 'Celebrities become so self-important they think that no one can cross them. There is an implicit feeling of arrogance that you can dress how you like, do what you like and treat people how you like. It is a sign of having made it. Photographers are frequent targets for this behaviour.'

It was not long before Victoria's aggressive stance towards cameramen began to rub off on David. Chris Neill noticed the changes almost as soon as Victoria arrived on the scene. His happy association with other United players remained the same, but an altercation outside the Reform Club in Manchester city centre in December 1998 made him realize that his formerly friendly relationship with United's number seven had gone for ever. It was the evening of the Manchester United Christmas Party, and the first time that he had photographed David and Victoria together. All the other players and their partners had posed happily for pictures, and when the star couple duly arrived he waited until Victoria, then heavily pregnant with Brooklyn, got out of their Range Rover, before taking three frames of the couple as they walked towards the club.

Their reaction was somewhat lacking in festive spirit. 'They both came up to me and started shouting, "Bastard, fuck off, get a life." All I had done was take their picture.'

It was an unpleasant shock for Chris. 'I was a United fan before David Beckham was born,' he says. 'The happiest day of my life was when I watched my team win the European Cup; so it comes as a jolt when your heroes behave so rudely.'

From that point on he began to get used to the abusive remarks and gestures that came his way whenever Beckham caught sight of him or his trademark white Fiesta. Chris was not the only one to suffer from Beckham's increasing suspicion of the media. On one occasion this proved expensive. Driving to the training ground one morning with Brooklyn in the back of his left-hand-drive Lincoln Navigator, David spotted an Italian film crew outside the ground. Distracted by their presence he failed to notice the Range Rover belonging to his team-mate Andy Cole. The cars were involved in a slow-motion head-on collision which was to cost Beckham several thousand pounds. Not that Cole, who has employed a chauffeur since losing his licence for a series of driving offences, seemed too concerned. His passion for driving has waned since he was forced to become a back-seat driver.

Beckham, on the other hand, has had a love affair with cars and speed ever since he could drive. Cars are, as he says, his 'pride and joy'. It would destroy him if he were unable to drive for any reason. He is like a Latin lover, falling for the curves and colours of one seductive sports car, only to discard her for another a few months later.

On one occasion he saw a two-tone silver and blue TVR sports car on the forecourt of a dealership in Alderley Edge. Like a child in a sweet shop, it seemed he had to have it whatever the cost. As the trade-in price he was offered for his Porsche seemed less than generous, he was counselled to go directly to the Blackpool-based manufacturers of the TVR. They hand-built the car in two weeks, fitting a special rear seat emblazoned with Brooklyn's name. But David soon discovered that the TVR is strictly for the enthusiast. The ride is hard and unforgiving, and after only a few hundred miles his love affair ended as abruptly as it had begun. And after all, why not? David justifies his passion: 'I like changing cars, and I suppose if I can afford to do it, I'll keep doing it. It isn't a crime to have a nice car.'

His first car was a humble Ford Escort, followed by a Volkswagen Golf. When he and other United youngsters like Nicky Butt and Gary Neville were given Honda Preludes as their first club cars, Beckham apparently irritated his manager by having his fitted – at his own expense – with leather upholstery and customized wheels. Always wanting to be different, always wanting to stand out from the crowd. Since then he has graduated to BMWs and Porsches and currently has an array of cars that include a Mercedes SLK, a Lincoln Navigator, a top-of-the-range Range Rover and a Ferrari 550 which Victoria bought him for his twenty-fourth birthday.

Something of a boy racer, he has talked about installing a quad bike track in the grounds of his new home and thoroughly enjoyed an afternoon's go-karting with the rest of the United team at an indoor track in Warrington. The players had been given special dispensation by Sir Alex Ferguson to take part in a potentially dangerous sport. Normally their contracts forbid them from indulging in hazardous activities such as skiing or riding motorbikes. For the moment David Beckham can only express his enthusiam for biking through fashion. Thus when Victoria was making her video to promote her solo single, he sported a yellow and black biker jacket emblazoned with the name of champion rider Kevin Schwantz.

While bike-riding remains a fantasy, he loves to drive his cars, and as a young man with superb reflexes he likes to drive fast, as his numerous driving offences attest. He has often been seen on the motorway talking on his mobile phone, and while he has never had a major accident his love of speed must worry Victoria, who would naturally be concerned that it could put his and Brooklyn's lives in danger.

In the old days booze and birds were the status symbols of successful sportsmen, George Best being the most notable example. These days fast cars seem to be the trophy of choice, particularly among young footballers. On match days Old Trafford is a veritable showroom for customized sports cars. The only thing that can slow these racers down would seem to be the law; and even then the club, which protects players and staff vigorously, does its best to shelter them.

Striker Dwight Yorke was banned for two months and fined £1,000 by Trafford magistrates for doing 120 miles an hour in his Ferrari Maranello on a stretch of the M56 in Hale, while his striking partner Andy Cole was disqualified for six months and fined £500 for speeding. In October 1999 manager Sir Alex Ferguson escaped a conviction when he convinced magistrates that he was driving on the hard shoulder of the M62 in his

BMW 750 in order to avoid a traffic jam because he had a severe bout of diarrhoea and needed to reach the Old Trafford toilets. On another occasion no one at the club would admit to driving a leased BMW 750 through a speed trap in Derbyshire. A charge against Sir Alex was dismissed, although the club was fined £650 with £35 costs for failing to name the driver.

In December 1999 it was David Beckham's turn. The previous July he had been caught exceeding the speed limit near his home in Alderley Edge, and now that his case was due to come before the magistrates he was a worried man. While he dreaded losing his licence – he had already accumulated ten points for previous convictions – he and his advisers had already put into effect plans to hire a full-time chauffeur.

However it soon became apparent that more was at stake here than a straightforward case of speeding. What happened that day in court, and the events that followed, shed a fierce light on to the nature of modern celebrity, the murky world of public relations and the way in which the media, the public and even the judiciary can be overawed by those who have enough fame and money. It is also an episode that reveals the consequences for those who get on the wrong side of this modern aristocracy.

In early December, a few days before Beckham's court case, Chris Neill and a fellow photographer were outside Old Trafford, waiting for midfielder Roy Keane. The protracted contract negotiations in which Keane had been embroiled were about to be resolved, and the *Daily Express* had commissioned Neill to take a picture of the Irish international. Neill's white Fiesta and his colleague's blue Mondeo were parked on the forecourt. As they waited, David Beckham marched up to Chris and launched into a torrent of abuse, then turned on his heel and left. Both photographers were shocked and bemused by his unprovoked tirade.

Days later, on Thursday 9 December 1999, Beckham stood before the magistrates at Stockport, Cheshire and explained why he had been caught by speed cameras driving at 76 m.p.h. on a 50 m.p.h. dual carriageway. He told the court that he had been 'intimidated and petrified' by an unidentified paparazzo photographer driving a white Ford Fiesta who trailed him for ten miles. During thirty-five minutes of sworn evidence, Beckham related how he had noticed the white Fiesta when he reached the end of the drive of his Alderley Edge home. The photographer had taken a picture, and then the white car had followed him. 'It was very close and I felt uncomfortable,' he said, adding that during the pursuit, the photographer had almost caused a serious accident as he had tried to overtake his £150,000 Ferrari to snatch another shot. 'He was swerving, taking pictures. He was not in control,' he said.

Concerned that his pursuer was more than simply an over-zealous cameraman, Beckham, who was on his way to join his team-mates for a pre-season friendly, decided to get away from him to prevent a serious accident. 'I was petrified,' he told the court. 'I felt intimidated. He was driving very dangerously and that scared me.' After driving twice round a roundabout to shake off the other car, Beckham put his foot down as he drove along the A74, which was where the police speed camera had caught him. Such was his concern that within two minutes of being caught, Beckham had phoned Wilmslow police station, Greater Manchester police headquarters and the force's traffic unit to explain his behaviour.

Beckham's defence immediately conjured up memories of Princess Diana's fatal accident in Paris, where she and her lover Dodi Fayed had been followed by paparazzi and the Mercedes they were travelling in was involved in a collision with a mysterious white Fiat Uno. When magistrates viewed the police video, they did see a white Ford pass by the camera eight seconds after Beckham. The driver has never been traced. The magistrates, however, were not convinced by Beckham's story, saying that his actions were 'unreasonable', while Manchester police confirmed that they had no evidence that the driver of a white Fiesta was harrassing him. Beckham was banned for eight months and fined £800, and immediately launched an appeal. So anxious was he about the ban that his solicitor, Nicholas Freeman, took the highly unusual step of going to a judge to ask for his licence back pending his appeal, which was set for the following Thursday, after the magistrates initially turned down the request.

As the media launched a hunt for the paparazzi photographer in the white Ford Fiesta, some people in Manchester guessed that the culprit had been Chris Neill. He was one of only two freelance photographers who regularly snapped local soccer stars. More than that, he had a white Fiesta.

Soon his phone was ringing red-hot. His mother Gladys asked him what on earth he was doing chasing a celebrity at high speed after what had happened to Princess Diana. His wife Adele was equally suspicious and accusing. She feared that no one would want to employ him once what he had done was exposed, and that they would have to sell their house. Even though he strenuously denied all knowledge of the incident, she remained sceptical.

Then the national newspapers began calling. They too took his denials with a pinch of salt. A reporter from the *Daily Mail* asked him how much he had earned from the photos of Beckham and wondered whether it had been worth the risk of chasing the football superstar at such high speed. He recalls: 'It was like being in the middle of a nightmare. I thought I would never work again unless I could prove where I was. Any moment I expected the police to come round and arrest me. It was a dreadful experience.'

His uncle, Fred Houghton, convinced of his nephew's innocence, worked himself into a fury over Beckham's defence, which could have such damaging consequences for his family. Such was his disgust at what he saw as the failure of the judicial process that Fred, a lifelong United supporter, vowed never to watch his team again. He did not have the chance to keep his word. Hours later, Fred Houghton died of a heart attack at the age of fifty-nine. 'Whether his fatal attack was triggered because he was so worked up about the Beckham court case, we'll never know,' said Chris.

As he tried to absorb the shocking news of his uncle's death, Chris was at the same time desperately trying to clear his name. He, his friends, and his family all believed that he would end up being tarred with the same brush as the paparazzi on the night Diana died. He was becoming increasingly frantic. He looked in his diary to see what he had been doing on that day back in July and suddenly saw that he had a cast-iron alibi.

On the day that David Beckham had allegedly been chased by a paparazzo in a white Ford Fiesta, Chris Neill was three thousand miles away, staying with a cousin at Niagara Falls in Canada with his five children. After this discovery he carried his passport with him to every job to prove to sceptics that he was not the culprit. Even so he took so much abuse that he decided to exchange his now notorious leased Fiesta for a red Mondeo. Looking back he says: 'It was a terrible experience for my family and myself, all the more so because of the death of my uncle. If I hadn't been in Canada and hadn't had my passport stamped my life would have been ruined.'

As Chris Neill licked his wounds, the Beckhams and their baby spent five hours Christmas shopping at Harrods, David once again hitting the headlines with his eccentric choice of headgear, a knitted Tibetan peasant's hat complete with bobble and ear flaps. It was a second shopping trip to the same store later that week, just forty-eight hours before he was due before a judge to ask for his driving ban to be quashed, which provided a further twist to the saga.

As on the previous Saturday, when they left the store they faced a dozen or more photographers waiting for them to get into their car. The routine was the same. They lingered in the store foyer, put on baseball caps and determinedly put their heads down so that the photographers would get a poor or unusable shot. As usual Victoria went ahead while David, carrying Brooklyn, and their bodyguard Mark Niblett followed behind. There was the usual brief mêlée as they pushed past the waiting snappers, Victoria thrusting one of them out of the way as she got into the car. Then the party drove off.

Those to whom I have spoken who witnessed the scene were astounded to see the banner headline 'Posh Baby Grab Terror' splashed across the following morning's *Sun*. The article, billed as an exclusive by the deputy showbiz editor, revealed how 'brave' Posh Spice had knocked a crazed fan to the ground as he tried to grab her son. The incident, which was quickly followed up by others in the media, was confirmed by the couple's spokeswoman, Caroline McAteer.

According to the story, the unidentified 'weirdo' had grabbed Brooklyn's arm and yelled: 'I just want a picture of me and Brooklyn together. Please, please let me.' Victoria was quoted as describing how she had pushed the man away from her 'like any mother'. The paper went on to say that the twenty-five-year-old singer admitted that she was scared and feared for her son's life. 'David and I were both shocked by the whole incident as any parent would be.'

Strangely, the incident was not captured on film either by the CCTV cameras outside Harrods or by the dozen or so photographers who had been within inches of their Mercedes car. A housewife who was quoted as a witness has proved untraceable. Strange, too, that the police, who had spent nearly a year investigating alleged death threats to the couple, were not immediately informed.

Could it have been a case of skilful spin-doctoring on the eve of David Beckham's appearance before a judge to win his licence back? As the *Guardian* newspaper noted: 'Headlines such as "Anger as Beckham escapes speeding by blaming

snappers" melted into "How Posh stopped baby-snatcher".
Beckham and Victoria were transformed from spoilt celebrities
into heroic parents.'

That same somewhat cynical stance was echoed by others
who had been close to the scene. Harrods media relations
officer Michael Mann said of the alleged assault: 'It was not
caught on security cameras and we have very good coverage. No
one saw it, not the doormen and not the photographers. In my
opinion it may not have happened and was possibly for the
papers.' One photographer who was there described the
incident as 'rubbish'. He went on: 'Nothing happened. Before
they came out they lingered in the foyer of door five. They
looked at us. They came out with caps pulled down over their
faces and heads down. A photographer got in the way; she
pushed him. David Beckham had a court case at the time. He
used the incident, spin-doctoring to get him off. There was no
manic fan. Victoria Beckham hasn't got the strength to push
anyone.' Similar views are held by their former bodyguard, who
had been with them both inside and outside the store. 'We
never even discussed it until the next day when it was in the
paper', he recalls. 'It was simply the fact that Victoria likes to get
the boot in with photographers and give them a hard time. She
hates the baby being photographed; it is her major concern.
David had the baby and was just getting into the car . . . She was
in one of her tempers and she lashed out at the photographers
who were there. Nobody saw anything, I certainly didn't see
anything and they didn't mention anything.'

As the nation pondered the latest threat to Brooklyn,
described by one media wit as the most famous infant since the
one born in Bethlehem two thousand years ago, his father
prepared to face Judge Barry Woodward, himself a collector of
classic cars, at Minshul Crown Court. During his sworn
testimony Beckham again argued that at the time of the offence
he was being trailed by a paparazzi photographer. Curiously, as

Beckham had to admit, none of the photographs supposedly taken by his alleged pursuer had ever been published, even though he agreed they would be worth a small fortune.

He was, however, quick to tell the court about the incident at Harrods. After informing the judge of another occasion, when he and Victoria had been followed by two carloads of photographers just before they were married, he went on to explain what had happened just days before as he left the Knightsbridge store. 'I was holding my baby boy and my wife was in front of me . . . as we walked out, someone lunged towards Brooklyn and me and my wife pushed them off and then we got into the back of the car.'

Speaking of the Harrods incident, his solicitor told the judge: 'It's difficult for anyone to understand what it is like to be in David Beckham's shoes. It's like a mass hysteria. He is always followed but in this instance it got out of hand. It was the straw that broke the camel's back.' At the end of the five-hour hearing, Judge Woodward took pity on Beckham, whom he described as an 'honest and truthful' witness, and handed back his licence. In his judgement he said that the case must be considered on its own particular merits. 'In effect, a burst of speed with the purpose of putting distance between himself and his pursuer does constitute a special reason,' he said.

He went on: 'Mr Beckham had a reasonable feeling that there could be a fifty miles-per-hour crash on a relatively busy road. He has had many incidents in which, by reason of his fame, he was pestered to such an extent he had cause to fear for his and his family's safety.' The decision caused outrage among motoring organizations.

Commentator Mark Lawson said in the *Guardian* immediately after the case: 'This feels like a landmark judgment. For the first time, the celebrity defence is enshrined in British law.' The celebrity defence – which dictates that the famous are held to different legal standards – originated in American courts and achieved its ultimate judgement in the case of O.J. Simpson, the Hollywood star who was controversially cleared of murdering his estranged wife and her companion.

Did David Beckham sincerely believe that he was being followed by a photographer in a white Ford Fiesta? Did he and Victoria genuinely believe that a maniac had tried to harm their son? Few others do, it seems.

It is inevitable that a certain amount of hype and spin should be part of the day-to-day life of modern celebrities, especially those as much in the public eye as David and Victoria Beckham. They are by no means unique. The exaggerated quote, the elaborate photo-call and the contrived story have all become part of the symbiotic relationship that exists between stars and the media. Bogus stories, like the one which produced the legendary tabloid headline, 'Freddie Starr Ate My Hamster', all add to the gaiety of nations, a surreal world where fact, fiction and fantasy collide. And yet the prevalence of spin in modern society, be it on behalf of politicians, royalty or pop singers, ultimately demonstrates a contempt for the public. Truth, however uncomfortable, becomes secondary to self-interest, however entertaining.

In an institution like the judiciary, where truth is the hand-maiden to justice, spin-doctoring ultimately has a corrupting effect on the legal process. Ultimately it is all about control. The sociology of spin, the ability to control what people think about a celebrity, a politician or even a government policy, invariably reflects the psychology of fame. Since the early days of Hollywood and the growth of mass entertainment, celebrities have tried to control and doctor their image. It is a state of mind that breeds a certain narcissism, a belief that everything must reflect their image and conform to their desires. Often this need for control can take on absurd proportions.

As psychologist Dr Glenn Wilson says: 'Stars become control freaks, hooked on publicity and power, manipulating the public for attention but vindictive against those whom they feel have unjustly obstructed or humiliated them.' An incident in March 2000, three months after the dust had settled on David Beckham's controversial court case, gives a revealing insight into this dark side of celebrity. When he was sensationally dropped by Alex Ferguson after missing training to be with his sick son, the spin doctors went into action, with the pro-Beckham media portraying the argument as a clash between a responsible new-age father on the one hand, and the unreasonable old-style dogma of the manager on the other.

Crucially the debate featured pictures of the errant player being ordered off the club's new training ground at Carrington by Sir Alex – pictures taken by Chris Neill. The publication of the photographs was beyond the control of either side and embarrassed the club and the manager and humiliated Beckham. A few weeks later Neill was waiting by traffic lights near the ground when David Beckham pulled up alongside him in his distinctive Lincoln Navigator. Beckham wound down his window and hurled a handful of stones at the photographer's car, breaking his passenger window. Then he ran the red light and drove off.

In a world where image is everything, Chris Neill had broken rule number one: he had presented the unvarnished truth.

Nine

Posh PLC

I T had been a light-hearted dinner party for the Princess of Wales; a glass of white wine, a plateful of Marks and Spencer's lasagne and the chance to chat with friends. As far as Diana was concerned, the evening, hosted by her friend, the newspaper heiress Kate Menzies, had given her an opportunity to escape her claustrophobic life at Kensington Palace. So it was a jolly Princess who emerged from the mews house where her detective Ken Wharfe waited for her. She was larking about with another of the guests, Major David Waterhouse of the Household Cavalry, trying to put a rubber balloon over his car exhaust. In a matter of minutes her carefree laughter would turn to tears.

Lurking in the shadows was a young paparazzo photographer who captured the potentially embarrassing scene of the Princess having fun with a young man who was certainly not her husband. The photographer was spotted and Diana's detective swiftly moved into action, apparently removing the film from the camera. Brushing aside tears of anger and frustration, Diana confronted the young cameraman, telling him that he and his sort were making her life a misery. 'I've been working hard all week,' she told him. 'It's the only time I've been out . . . I've got so few friends left and this will only make things worse for me.'

When the story broke in the autumn of 1987, the photographer, twenty-two-year-old Jason Fraser, became that week's hate figure in the mass media. He was dubbed 'the man who made the fairytale princess cry'. While his exposure in the popular press disconcerted him, it did not deter him. Almost until the day she died, Jason Fraser stalked the Princess, snapping her around London and on holiday. Of all the paparazzi, it was Jason Fraser whom she feared most – and with good reason. Charming, bilingual and articulate, Fraser does not conform to the public's image of a photographer 'stalker' of the stars. Over the last decade he and other paparazzi have built a tightly-knit group who target the playgrounds of the rich and famous. It was he who organized the selling and distribution of the now infamous pictures of Diana kissing her lover Dodi Fayed during her last holiday in the Mediterranean on board the *Jonikal,* the yacht owned by Dodi's father, Harrods boss Mohammed al Fayed.

Ironically, since Diana's death, Fraser has scored a major coup with grainy holiday shots of Prince Charles's partner, Camilla Parker Bowles, as well as other celebrities such as model Claudia Schiffer, comedian Rory Bremner and singer and actress Madonna. Like a modern-day big game hunter, this doyen of the paparazzi has boasted of the adrenalin rush he gets from each exclusive celebrity 'kill', in particular the buzz he experiences hanging out of helicopters with his long lens. Ruthless, well-connected and highly successful, Fraser does admit to having his own self-imposed code of ethics. 'I would never do to anybody what I wouldn't want done to myself,' he once said.

Fraser happened to fly back on the same plane as the Beckhams after their honeymoon, sitting two rows behind them on their British Airways flight from Nice to Heathrow. He watched as David fed the baby, changed his nappy, and soothed him when he cried. Later he watched as Brooklyn vomited over his father's blue linen shirt. Afterwards he said, somewhat disingenuously, 'Seeing Posh, Becks and Brooklyn was one of the most enchanting sights I have ever seen.' By a sublime twist of fate, the king of the paparazzi, the man who had made the life of Diana, Princess of Wales so difficult, was about to become the unofficial 'By Appointment' photographer to the new royal family.

This arrangement would add a further dimension to the dynamic that exists between celebrities, paparazzi and the public. Before Diana's death, the public, for all their gripes about the content of the tabloid press, nevertheless enjoyed the vicarious thrill of seeing stars 'off duty' and going about their private lives. While they may have criticized the underhand methods employed to catch celebrities off their guard, they loved the end result. Hence the rise in the circulation figures of those newspapers which published the infamous photos of Sarah, Duchess of York having her toes sucked by John Bryant, or the no less invasive shots of Princess Diana with Dodi Fayed.

Since Diana's death, however, the role of the paparazzi has come under intense and hostile scrutiny. The British media have taken steps to clean up their act with a self-policed code of conduct. The use of intrusive pictures, particularly of children, has been widely condemned.

So what have the stars and their photographer stalkers done? Welcome to the world of the paparazzi photo-call. As in the bad old days, this new generation of photographs look for all the world like casual, unposed snaps of stars at play. The celebrity subjects seem oblivious to the presence of the camera, the settings seem impromptu, the pictures themselves invariably fresh and revealing. Unlike more formal arrangements, such as the annual photo-call of the royal family enjoying themselves on the ski slopes, there seems to be nothing staged about these paparazzi pictures.

And yet far from being spontaneous, the paparazzi photo opportunity is as contrived an event as a first-night celebrity party. The paparazzi are contacted in advance by the stars or by their agents, a suitable deal is struck and photos are taken which make it appear that the subject has been caught unawares.

Everyone is happy. The public think they are being given a secret, unauthorized glimpse into the private lives of the stars. The magazines and newspapers are able to feed that illusion and increase their circulations as a result. The celebrities themselves profit either financially or through publicity or both, and the photographer takes informal pictures without the hassle of stalking an unwilling quarry. As one senior newspaper executive admitted: 'We get revealing pictures and the stars get publicity, a free holiday and a few grand in their back pockets.' In a way, it is a natural development of the notion of 'infotainment'; the meshing of fact and fantasy, entertainment and news, which is subsequently passed off as real life.

Few celebrities will admit to being willing participants in such an arrangement, and most resent any implication that they would be party to such collusion. Victoria is no exception. When she and her sister Louise were driving to the opening of a new Thai restaurant in Knightsbridge at the end of London Fashion Week, several paparazzi received calls to tell them of their impending arrival. After they were photographed, Victoria complained to the restaurant, accusing them of tipping off the media. Suggestions made on the ITV news programme *Tonight With Trevor McDonald* that she or Louise had engineered similar tip-offs were hotly denied by the singer. 'That really upsets me,' she stated. 'If my sister did that, you'd think they'd get something more juicy and accurate, wouldn't you?'

In a conversation with writer Mike Pattenden, David has also disputed the notion that he had encouraged media interest by actively courting the press. He pointed out that their chat was only the fifth interview he had given in two years, and said that, apart from the famous £1 million wedding pictures sold to *OK!* magazine, he had never been paid for any press.

That interview took place at the end of March 2000, a few days after he had had his famous blond locks shaved off for a Number Two haircut costing £300. His usual stylist Tyler had travelled to Goff's Oak from the Knightsbridge salon of Vidal Sassoon to give him that masculine, rather aggressive haircut. When word leaked out that the man once known as 'Pretty Boy' had changed his look so dramatically, fans scoured the dustbins in the hope of finding a lock of his shorn hair as a souvenir.

Nor was David the only one to get the chop. Brooklyn was given a similar skinhead cut, while Victoria had her hair coloured blonde by Yotis, the head colourist at Vidal Sassoon. Everyone was clamouring for pictures of the family's fresh, radical look, with sub-editors salivating at the prospect of writing the headline: 'Short Beck and sides'. Unknown to the waiting photographers who were camped outside the house in Goff's Oak, the Beckhams had other ideas.

They had a meeting planned with their new paparazzo acquaintance, Jason Fraser. For it to be successful, they had to avoid the presence of other photographers. David religiously kept on his trademark baseball cap to hide his sharp new haircut from prying lenses. A call to the local constabulary ensured that they were on hand to stop any tailing paparazzi, and the Beckhams made good their escape from Goff's Oak.

Nevertheless, a green Subaru filled with photographers slipped through the police cordon and set off in pursuit. When they reached Piccadilly in central London a handy Securicor van driver was commandeered to help. As his van was in front of the photographers' car in a narrow one-way street he was asked if he would stop to allow the Beckhams, who were in front of him, to lose them. The impromptu plan worked perfectly. The driver stopped at the T-junction, successfully blocking the road and preventing the paparazzi from following any further.

A few minutes later the couple pulled into the NCP car park close to Harrods, where Jason Fraser was waiting. He needed only a moment to take the shots. As the light in the car park was poor, he asked them to cross the road outside with baby Brooklyn, and then to lose themselves inside Harrods for a few hours in order to give him time to sell the exclusive pictures. So the couple went through their paces, their unsmiling faces giving the impression of uncomfortable irritation at the presence of a photographer, and Fraser duly sold the snaps to *OK!* and the *Sun*. Rumours abounded in the tabloid world that Fraser had paid them on this and on other occasions a substantial part of the money he received for these photos.

When the pictures were published the issue of money became a major talking point for quite another reason. Beckham had famously signed a lucrative sponsorship deal with the makers of Brylcreem hair products, and some commentators were quick to condemn his lack of commercial sense, arguing that the loss of his longer hair would be certain to jeopardize his deal. Victoria took the trouble to phone a radio station to pour scorn on this idea. 'David has not lost any money from Brylcreem,' she told them. 'So when you said he has no brain for shaving off his hair because he would lose four million pounds, you were wrong. He has not lost a penny. I would go crazy if he lost four million pounds by having his hair cut.' The couple's own spin on the haircut saga was that David had shaved his head because he was tired of fans imitating his look. In any event, financial analysts valued his Brylcreem deal at £200,000, a fraction of the reported figure. 'He's a professional sportsman, not a model,' a friend was quoted as saying, ironically just as David was posing in a range of designer gear for a men's glossy magazine.

Interestingly, his Brylcreem contract was due to be renegotiated shortly before he cut his hair. No less curious, in the Fraser photographs, he was seen in a £100 white Tommy Hilfiger T-shirt at a time when the trendy clothing company were considering a sponsorship deal with the Manchester United star.

The couple's next liaison with their favourite paparazzo came in May 2000 when David organized a 'surprise' holiday for Victoria, flying her to a secluded villa in Tuscany. Only it was

no surprise to Jason Fraser who happily organized pictures of
the couple for *OK!* and the *Sun* as well as for foreign magazines.
This time Victoria's agent, Alan Edwards of the Outside
Organisation, liaised with the photographer and the media.

And the media wanted more. *OK!* offered £100,000 for
pictures of their trip to Los Angeles a few days later, where
Victoria was due to team up with the well-known American
songwriter Rhett Lawrence, who has written for Whitney
Houston, Mel C and Christina Aguilera, to pen lyrics for her
debut solo album.

Jason Fraser was sitting nearby when the Beckhams boarded
their Upper Class Virgin flight at Heathrow on Sunday 7 May.
Just like real royalty, however, there was no question of
fraternization with the media. This was business, not friendship.
Victoria and David were deeply uncomfortable at the prospect
of being discovered associating with the king of the paparazzi.
Nor was the smooth-talking Fraser, who is widely admired for his
intrepid skills at hiding in bushes or behind windbreaks, keen
to be unmasked as going 'straight'. Both parties preferred to
keep their dealings at a distance, the Beckham's agent Alan
Edwards or their bodyguard Mark Niblett acting as the buffer
between them. Indeed, Victoria was irritated that Fraser had
been on the same flight as they had and stayed in the same
hotel, the five-star Peninsula in Beverly Hills. She insisted that
any photo shoot be completed in the first couple of days of their
holiday to give her time to relax.

Their plan ran into problems from the start. First they were
snapped at LA Airport by a rival American photographer. Then,
while the couple were walking around Bloomingdale's store at
the Beverly Centre mall with Fraser snapping away, a security
guard, unaware that the whole enterprise was an elaborate set-
up, threatened to throw the paparazzo out for harassing these
celebrity shoppers. Besides, while pictures of Brooklyn taking
packs of Ralph Lauren boxer shorts were all very well, Fraser

wanted more intimate poses from the famously sulky couple. After some tetchy negotiations, they agreed to stage a photo call by the fountain outside their hotel.

It was a Royal Command Performance with a difference. The 'royal couple' posed at the direction of their tame paparazzo, kissing and cuddling by the fountain and kicking a football to toddler Brooklyn. When Victoria, wearing a white vest emblazoned with the words 'Rock Star', left them to join her songwriting team, David and his son, with bodyguard and photographer in tow, visited Disneyland.

Finally Fraser left them in peace. Before he returned to Britain to sell the shots, however, he asked the Beckhams to keep out of sight. He was particularly worried about David's plans to visit his favourite basketball team, the LA Lakers, fearing that if he was pictured attending the game it would dilute the exclusivity, and hence the price, of his own set of photographs. David ignored the request, such is his passion for the sport and for his team, who were in the national play-off finals. He attended the match, where he was was thrilled to meet stars such as Dustin Hoffman, Jack Nicholson, and German soccer ace Jurgen Klinsmann.

Meanwhile Victoria was equally happy, inspired by the love songs, most of them concerning her relationship with her husband, she had written. To cap a successful week, their spokeswoman, Caroline McAteer faxed to their hotel a copy of the *Sun* in which Fraser's pictures appeared, complete with the front page headline 'Beck in the USA'.

Victoria has consistently emphasized how important it is to maintain her son's privacy. 'He is the one thing in our lives that is private,' she has said. 'That's why it is upsetting when people said I was planning to make money out of selling pictures of him. We have never intended to do that.' On another occasion she said, 'Brooklyn won't do any pictures until he is big enough to decide what he wants to do or doesn't want to do. He's not a money-spinner. People were saying: "They left the hospital with their little asset", and that really hurt a lot.'

Fraser was once more helpfully on hand to record the couple's visit with Brooklyn to their local zoo in August 2000, pictures of which appeared in the Sunday papers days before the release of Victoria's first solo single. A far cry, some uncharitable critics would say, from their avowed intent to keep Brooklyn away from the cameras.

While Victoria should be admired for the skill with which she has managed her fame and that of David and Brooklyn, their fans might welcome a little more honesty about their relationship with the press. They have made plain their views on what they regard as media harassment. Many would sympathize with David when he says: 'When the media intrudes into your private life and makes you have to change the way you live, I think the press has gone too far.' Certainly they have support from their celebrity friends. When pictures were taken of David and Victoria sunbathing by the pool at Elton John's villa in the south of France during their courtship, the singer made an official protest to the Press Complaints Commission. The PCC upheld his complaint, agreeing in their adjudication that the pictures, published in the *Daily Star*, had been intrusive.

Victoria's fellow Spice Girl Melanie Chisholm added her voice to those who believed that the nation was displaying an unhealthy interest in the Beckhams, maintaining that their private life had become the focus of an obsession equal to that of Princess Diana and Dodi Fayed. 'We don't have Princess Diana to follow around any more, so people have picked on her [Victoria],' she said; remarks that Diana's mother Frances Shand Kydd regarded as 'hurtful' and 'insulting', responding with, 'There is a great deal of difference between being a showbusiness personality and a princess.'

Ironically, Victoria uses the 'Diana' defence to justify her dealings with the press. She argues that in a world where pursuing paparazzi will go to such dangerous lengths to snatch 'that picture' of a celebrity, it is occasionally necessary to allow privileged access to selected snappers in order to safeguard their privacy and security the rest of the time.

What neither Victoria nor David mentions is whether the rumours are correct that they make money from these secret deals and whether there is any conflict between what they say in public and what they negotiate in private. Yet the apparent contradiction between their complaints about the press on the one hand and their willingness to use the media on the other does little to help the important debate which is currently raging about public figures, their right to privacy and the limits of permissible intrusion. The government is considering legislation on this issue, an issue which came even more to the fore in the summer of 2000 when the Prime Minister's own family became a media target, first with stories about his teenage son, Euan, and then with pictures of his baby Leo's christening.

Tony Blair, who had expressly asked for press discretion on this intimate family occasion, described the publication of the christening pictures as a gross invasion of privacy. When *Heat* magazine asked Victoria to comment on Blair's distress, she was dismissive of his reaction, saying that she had had to put up with much worse, including one front page photograph which had shown Brooklyn completely naked. 'He's only realized it's a bad thing now it's happened to him, but this sort of thing has been happening for years,' she said. 'Now that it's happened to his son something might change at last. It's about time we had decent privacy laws in this country. I'm not complaining about the attention I get because I ask for that, but my family doesn't.'

Some might feel that her remark was as hyprocritical as it was disingenuous, her own role in organizing photo-calls of herself, her husband and son and selling the pictures for six-figure sums to celebrity magazines only making it harder for others, be they pop stars or politicians, to insist on their privacy being respected by the mass media. In some respects it is easy to see Victoria's point of view. If pictures of her and her family sell newspapers, why should they not be the ones to take the lion's share of the money? If fame is a commodity, why should the paparazzi get pictures of them for free, when every snatched shot is 'stealing' a slice of that fame. But their actions are based on a double standard. They want to have their media cake and eat it. They complain about intrusion into their lives and that of their son and yet when it suits them they engineer that very same intrusion, exploiting their own privacy for publicity and profit.

The issue of double standards aside, in many ways the couple, particularly Victoria, are very clear-eyed and businesslike in trying to make the most of their commercial potential. She recognizes that they only have a short shelf-life and she does not want to fritter away the slightest opportunity. Companies see them simply as marketing tools to sell their goods – so why shouldn't they do the same? Better that they themselves should profit from their own fame than that others should simply make money at their expense.

Since famously selling their wedding pictures to *OK!* for £1 million, the Beckhams have cashed in regularly through their connection with the celebrity magazine. For their part the magazine's owners, Northern and Shell, are keen both to exploit and to protect their circulation golden goose. There is speculation that publisher Richard Desmond, who made his fortune producing top-shelf girlie magazines, aims to promote a 'Posh and Becks' brand, selling a variety of merchandise, including the possibility of Posh perfume and cosmetics as well as a pyjama range endorsed by Brooklyn. The couple, it is said, have set up a company, VDB – the initials of Victoria, David and Brooklyn – to manage the licensing venture, and are following in the paths of American stars like basketball player Michael

Jordan who have made millions from the value of their names. There is talk of a chain of Posh and Becks restaurants, calendars, film projects and even a David Beckham football school. Such is the need to protect the Posh and Becks brand that when Northern and Shell discovered that I was writing a book on the Beckhams they sent threatening legal letters to myself and to employees at my publishers, Michael O'Mara Books.

While the Posh and Becks brand has mainly national appeal, an internet deal to sell David Beckham's own brand of sports gear and games is on the cards to tap his huge international potential. His decision to front the dotcom venture will, according to financial analysts, net him £1 million and a 2.75 per cent stake in the concern, far more than any of the other sporting personalities, including Michael Owen, Alan Shearer and boxer Prince Naseem Hamed, who have also been lined up for the website.

The deal, negotiated between his manager Tony Stephens and the boss of Harvey Nichols, would move David ahead of his wife in the earnings stakes if it reaches its full potential. As one financial observer noted: 'David is already a massive name, but he's not yet capitalized on his popularity around the world.'

They are inundated with offers on an almost daily basis. One moment David is considering an approach to front the launch of a breakfast cereal, the next they are talking about appearing naked in *Playboy*. There seems to be no limit to the financial horizons for the Beckhams to explore, a remarkable achievement for a couple still in their mid-twenties. Much of the credit is due to Victoria, whose keen eye for a deal and ruthless exploitation of her status is matched only by her ambition for herself and her family. Never content with her social position, watchful and at times envious of the achievements of others, she is the commercial dynamo that drives the Posh and Becks machine.

As the music critic Ray Connolly has observed of her: 'Driven by ambition, she has a gift for marketing, a genius for selling herself. If she hadn't become a pop singer she would almost certainly have found some other way to make her millions. She's a born entrepreneur, endlessly offering up some new product to the all-buying consumer.'

The girl who was once on the dole is rather proud of the fact that in the league tables of richest young entertainers she stands out way in front with a fortune estimated at £24 million. It gives her quiet satisfaction to know that she is considered to be the most financially astute and marketable of the Spice Girls. She is particularly pleased that singer Geri Halliwell, formerly Ginger Spice, who split from the all-girl band on the brink of a lucrative American tour, is valued at a mere £17.2 million. As for her husband David, he is number 21 in the charts, worth an estimated £5 million, just behind tennis player Tim Henman and Liverpool soccer ace Robbie Fowler.

Like many self-made millionaires she displays a curiously contradictory attitude towards money. She is happy to spend £15,000 on clothes in a morning but at the same time she will scrimp on a tip to the taxi driver. The daughter of a self-employed businessman, she describes herself as a 'tight arse' and with good reason.

Not only is she careful with her millions, she is acutely aware that her name and status can help secure discounts with those who supply goods and services. She has said with obvious pride that one of the best things about being famous is that she gets a thirty per cent discount from Gucci. And just as Sarah, Duchess of York, notoriously haggled with traders when she was furnishing her new house, so Victoria Beckham has few qualms about negotiating deals.

British Airways found that she was no push-over when her luggage was stolen whilst returning from Miami to Manchester after recording the latest Spice Girls album. Four Louis Vuitton suitcases containing toys, her song-lyric book – later returned – and numerous specially made designer dresses went missing. Victoria was furious about the theft, all the more so as she arrived home with little to wear. 'I literally didn't have anything else to wear – not even a pair of knickers,' she claimed. 'All my favourite clothes were in those bags.' The airline paid a high price for upsetting the formidable Mrs Beckham.

Yet hard-headed as she may be when it comes to business, from time to time she shows a softer, more sentimental side. Just after Christmas 1999, she and her sister Louise went shopping to Tesco and Marks and Spencer in Alderley Edge. During the trip the diamond from her £40,000 engagement ring fell out, possibly when she caught her hand on the metal mesh of her shopping trolley. Even though they were offered a £5,000 reward, security staff never found the missing stone. While she was deeply upset about the loss, she expressed the wish that a homeless person had found it and used the money to buy themselves a house. The plight of the homeless is constantly on her mind, especially when she is driving through central London, which at times resembles a refugee camp, such are the numbers and the variety of homeless people, particularly the young, sheltering in doorways. Before she gets into her chauffeur-driven Mercedes she will often give a ten- or a twenty-pound note to a homeless youngster if she sees one near the recording studio she and the Spice Girls use in Whitfield Street in the West End. In an exclusive interview with *The Big Issue*, the street magazine sold by homeless people, she admitted that their problems struck a chord: 'I still feel quite guilty about spending [money],' she said. 'It's hard to justify spending five thousand pounds on a coat when there are people living rough on the streets.'

She is not quite the misery-guts she would like to pretend – even to the much-derided media. When she was being interviewed by one journalist at Alderley Edge, she invited the non-driving scribe to join her in her chauffeur-driven car back to London. On her birthday it has become something of a ritual for her to visit local hospitals and hand out her cake to youngsters in the children's ward. She finds a charitable use, too, for her unwanted designer clothes. After her sister and other members of her family have rummaged through them, they are put into black plastic bin-liners and sent to the local charity shop at Goff's Oak. 'She is very generous,' one charity worker said. 'People think she is stuck up but they don't see the other side of her.'

Even though she was driven to school in a Rolls-Royce, Victoria knew both rejection and failure before she found fame with the Spice Girls, an experience which has made her all the more keenly aware of the pleasures of success. In contrast, while David is a working-class boy from a modest background, success has literally been at his feet throughout his teenage and adult life. Cocooned inside the Manchester United institution since he was sixteen, he consequently has very little concept of the true value of money. Ironically the working-class boy made good behaves more like royalty than his wife as far as finances are concerned. For him, money is simply a prop in the theatre of life. While Victoria is calculating, he is carefree. 'It's the one thing David and I differ on,' says Victoria. 'He never looks at the price of anything.' He seems happy to let her apply the brakes to his spending, even when it applies to his passion for cars. 'If she doesn't want me to have it, she just phones [the suppliers] up and cancels it,' he admits.

Though they approach the notion of wealth by different paths, they have both arrived at the same location, the undisputed king and queen of conspicuous consumption. While the House of Windsor stands by the values of duty, a wider obligation to society, and a virtuous frugality, this new royal family worships at the altars of extravagance and indulgence. Gucci, Prada and Donna Karan are their gods.

Virtually every day they pay obeisance at their shrines to shopping; the Trafford Centre in Manchester, Knightsbridge in London. They will spend in an hour what some people earn in a year, lavishing thousands of pounds on jewellery, clothes and cars. In 1999, David was known to spend around £66,000 a month on everything from private jets, first-class flights, watches and sports cars.

Like the aristocracy of a bygone age, they are eager to display their wealth. 'It's absolutely gorgeous,' boasted Victoria when she showed off the £50,000 black diamond ring which David bought her for their first anniversary. It neatly matched the £30,000 earrings he had surprised her with on her twenty-sixth birthday.

As psychologist Dr Glenn Wilson observes: 'Their endless shopping trips are a need to remind themselves that they have made it, that they are successful. For them, wealth is a new idea, and their addiction to consumption reveals a couple of limited scope and imagination. Quite simply they are doing what many people dream about if they won the lottery: big house, flash cars and everything money can buy.'

Since becoming a national institution, however, they have begun to move in the social stratosphere where money becomes secondary to status. Their holidays are an indication of the extent to which they have truly made it. Just as the young royals spend their vacations at the villa homes of their rich and famous friends, so the Beckhams are following in their wake. They have been frequent guests of Elton John's, while Lord Lloyd Webber invited them to stay at his villa during their honeymoon.

This summer they crowned their rise to the summit of the nation's *nouveaux riches* when the Harrods owner, Mohammed al Fayed invited them to his villa in the south of France. During their week-long stay they joined al Fayed on board the same yacht on which he had entertained Princess Diana and his son Dodi in the summer of 1997, shortly before their deaths. A friend was quoted as saying: 'He is used to entertaining royalty at his home, and it's fair to say David and Victoria were treated like a prince and princess.'

For once no photographer was on hand to capture their enthronement.

Ten

What She Really, Really Wants

S HE didn't want to go, she really, really didn't want to go. In fact what she really, really wanted was to stay at home. That much was utterly clear. A clear sign of her nervousness was her language. Normally it was one colour. Blue. Today it was deep blue, her apprehension was mixed with real fear and resentment, resentment at the hidden stalker who had the one thing she hates to give up: control.

The horrible threats had unnerved her so much that ever-professional Victoria could have been excused for wanting to pull out of the annual Brit Awards where she and the remaining Spice Girls were due to be presented with a Lifetime's Achievement award. In the days before the prestigious ceremony, held at London's Earls Court, she had been sent a sick letter containing a newspaper photograph of her, altered to show blood spurting from a bullet hole in her head and the chilling warning: 'You are going to get yours.' This latest threat, which was immediately sent to the police for forensic tests, contained the date, March 3, 2000 – the night of the Brit Awards. What Victoria didn't realize was that former Spice Girl and now arch-rival, Geri Halliwell had received a similar threat.

Onlookers could have mistaken her edginess for stage fright or prima-donna behaviour when Victoria Beckham joined the rest of the Spice Girls for several hours of rehearsals before that evening's gala event. Her reflex aggression, the usual sign that she is trying to disguise her nervousness was apparent to those who had to deal with her. As she was walking off stage after the rehearsal, someone in the gantry shone a powerful red laser pen at her, the beam hitting her on the shoulder. For all Victoria knew it could have been an assassin armed with a rifle mounted with laser sights. She was absolutely terrified and was immediately hustled away by a mob of security guards and taken to her private dressing room. Senior police officers climbed the gantry in a vain search for the intruder, while back in her dressing room Victoria waited nervously.

As the girls were the last act to perform, Victoria had several long hours to kill, anxious minutes of worrying and waiting. By the time she and the other girls went on stage to collect the award from Hollywood actor Will Smith and sing a medley of their hits, Victoria was in pieces. Just before their entrance there was a commotion in the audience as Geri Halliwell made a dramatic exit, a phalanx of dark-suited minders clearing a path through the astonished audience. No one knew of the death threat to Geri and many must have thought her departure a direct snub to the other Spice Girls. She had already caused quite a stir, not only with an overt performance of her new single, 'Bag It Up', which offended Victoria with its pointed references to independent women and shopping trolleys, but also because she had refused to join the Spice Girls on stage to collect their award.

Victoria appeared not to notice Geri's exit as she, Mel C, Mel B and Emma went through their routine, and as the words of their final song 'Goodbye' echoed round the hall, many in the audience thought that this was their swan song. As they reached their finale, the stage was shaken with a series of explosions and the audience were treated to an unexpected fireworks display. It was too much for Victoria. It seemed she hadn't been told about the surprise ending and in her acute apprehensive state presumably thought a bomb had gone off nearby. The singer, her heart in her mouth, collapsed in tears and had to be helped off the stage by her colleagues. Members of the audience, thinking that she was overcome by the emotion of the evening, simply applauded her and the other girls all the louder. She recovered enough composure to bravely give a number of brief TV and radio interviews and joined David and her family for the Spice Girls party afterwards.

It's unlikely that she gave much thought to Geri Halliwell's sudden departure from the auditorium. It is no secret that since the split in 1998, just before their huge American tour, Geri has been *persona non grata* to Victoria. Indeed when Elton John smilingly asked her what she thought of Geri during a TV show, Victoria was simply lost for words, hardly daring to speak lest she launch into a torrent of abuse.

The first indications that all was not well was when Geri failed to appear with the rest of the Spice Girls on the National Lottery TV show on 28 May 1998. Hiding her anger and sense of rejection, Victoria said diplomatically, 'Geri is feeling poorly at the moment.' But she added, 'I felt very lonely after she'd gone.' It turned out that Geri was disillusioned and exhausted. They had all exchanged strong words about the way the band was going on their journey back from a gig in Helsinki and Geri had made no secret of the fact that she had been discussing her future career plans in TV with Chris Evans.

A strong-minded firebrand, Geri had been the *de facto* manager since the split with Simon Fuller. Could the Spice Girls survive as a foursome? The next gig on the Scandinavian leg of the tour was in Oslo and the four girls went on stage without her. The prestigious tour of America now looked to be in jeopardy. Victoria's considered reaction to Geri's departure expressed her sense of rejection and confusion, 'I really miss Geri a lot. I was really upset and gutted. The next minute I wanted to punch her in the head. We'll get through it. I got on really well with Geri and I really like her.' While her professional life was traumatic, it wasn't all doom and gloom for Victoria. She had just become an aunt, her sister Louise, twenty-one, giving birth to a baby girl, Liberty.

However June 1998 was a challenging month for both Victoria and David in more ways than one. While she was representing Britain in America, he was playing for England in the World Cup '98. Victoria's reviews were somewhat better than David's following his sending off for kicking Argentinian player, Diego Simeone, in a fit of temper on the pitch at St Étienne. When England was down to ten men and lost the game on penalties, he was universally blamed for England being knocked out of the cup and he was dubbed Public Enemy Number One. The first thing the devastated and shamed David did when he sat alone in the dressing room was to phone Victoria. Then he followed the advice of his boss, Alex Ferguson, and sought the company of the one person he loved the most, flying to New York to Victoria's uncritical embrace.

On 15 June the remaining Spice Girls triumphantly launched their American tour in Miami and during the two-hour concert Geri's name was not mentioned once. The others covered her vocal duties seamlessly. Victoria said proudly, 'Luckily America went exceptionally well. It could really have been a bad time for us and there were a lot of people trying to be negative. And now I feel a bit sorry for Geri.' The American tour was very gruelling with venues in the middle of nowhere and long journeys in between. Victoria found it especially difficult. She had just discovered that she was pregnant and was unlucky enough to suffer with regular morning sickness. However, the show would go on, a determined Victoria would not bow out of their forthcoming sell-out dates at Wembley Stadium.

Since the departure of Geri the band have grown and developed in other ways, not all of them musical. The birth of Brooklyn and Mel B's daughter, Phoenix Chi, as well as Victoria's well-publicized marriage indicated that the days of the Spice Girls were drawing to a close. These young brash women who had taken Britain by storm in the mid-1990s were now mature, responsible adults, as concerned about changing nappies and feeding babies as going out clubbing and cutting loose.

On the surface things were still fine. When they were recording their third album in the famous Abbey Road studios in north London in the autumn of 1999, the girls seemed to be having fun. Victoria, as usual, brought along bags of crisps and sweets for the girls and the recording crew as well as bottles of cheap 'champagne', Asti Spumante, which the girls used to drink before they became famous. The drink has become a tradition; they still drink it when they are together now to remind them of the good old days. But this time she brought more than refreshments. She carried Brooklyn into the studios, leaving him sleeping with a similarly comatose Phoenix Chi in a makeshift crèche filled with toys that she brought with her.

The girls met up with Rodney Jerkins, the black American songwriter who was producing the album. It is said that the hard-working American can be an intimidating character. Naturally the girls knew he was good and everyone wanted to do well. Victoria may have been more nervous than the others, aware that her voice is the weakest of the quartet. Doubtless she didn't want to let the others down. So she will have been delighted when he heaped fulsome praise on her and the other girls about their work. It really broke the ice and from then on the girls joshed Jerkins mercilessly about his diet – apparently he eats about six hamburgers a day – his heavy gold jewellery, in fact anything they could think of. He and his team teased the girls right back and, much to the amusement of studio technicians, over the weeks a relationship of mutual sarcasm and respect developed.

David spent as much time as he could spare in the recording studios, playing with baby Brooklyn and listening to the girls. After each recording session he would be quick to bolster Victoria's confidence, telling her how good she was. His encouragement and support has played a large part in convincing her to continue in the pop world after doubting her own abilities. As he said recently in an interview with *OK!* magazine, 'I think there was a period of self-doubt because she hadn't done anything for about six to eight months. Brooklyn had just been born, we'd got married, we'd done the family thing by being together – and people were starting to notice that the other girls were bringing out solo things and Victoria wasn't.'

The Spice Girls continue to support each other too. So they all went along to the Round House in London's Camden Town to support Mel B who nervously paraded down the catwalk during a fashion show and they all turned up for a concert in Sheffield when Mel C launched her first solo single. No doubt when Geri pipped Emma and the band she was singing with, Tin Tin Out, to the number one slot, Victoria will have contacted and consoled her blonde friend.

Inevitably though tensions inside the group were mounting as they all tried to pursue their own solo careers whilst remaining loyal to the band. Mel C was first to break cover, admitting that there was some friction between the girls. She said, 'There are rows and ructions in the band every other day.' Perhaps the others in the band felt some resentment now that Victoria was the most photographed woman in Britain and Mel C made it clear that she disapproved of her lavish lifestyle when she criticized the wedding as 'over the top'.

It was noticeable that when she made her controversial debut on the catwalk none of the other Spice Girls were there to watch her. 'That was a pretty clear message,' one music associate was quoted as saying.

Inside the industry rumours were rife that a band, long past the normal sell-by date for pop groups, were on the verge of splitting up. There were even calls led by pop pundit Jonathan King for the girls to call it a day and go their own way. Stories circulated suggesting that band members failed to appear for meetings and even recording sessions. There were other tensions. When the band convened in London for a private meeting with record industry executives and their advisers to discuss the future of the band, Mel C didn't turn up. After this meeting, the rumour mill churned out endless stories saying that the girls had split up. It is true that when the girls were finishing off recording their third album in Miami, Mel C did not join the others. She flew in after they had left to lay down her vocals to songs that the rest of the band had already recorded.

At the same time, whatever their personal differences, they had contractual obligations to meet. An eight-concert tour in Manchester and London in December 1999 was a sell-out and they spent weeks rehearsing at Elstree Studios in Hertfordshire. Nothing seemed to go right for them and Victoria complained about everything from the choreography to the organization. While the concerts were well received, there wasn't the vitality or commitment of old. Critics noted Victoria's unwillingness to participate in the band's on-stage antics during their opening concert in Manchester in December 1999. It was felt that Victoria's heart might not be in it any more, her famous enigmatic aloofness making her look 'oddly detached' from the others. Now she was a wife and a mother, the Girl Power thing had worn thin.

At the end of each concert in Manchester, rather than stay for an after-show drink with the rest of the band and production crew, it was noticed that Victoria and Mel C left as soon as they had taken their bows on stage. It seemed that Victoria felt that she had grown up, grown away from the larking-about, acting-the-fool all-girl band. Every performance it was the same story, last to arrive, first to leave.

Even their solid fan base seemed to be dwindling. Since their debut as complete unknowns at the Brits only three years before they have racked up no less than eight UK number one singles, two smash hit platinum albums, selling 35 million albums and 24 million singles worldwide. In the ephemeral world of pop that counts for nothing, the teenage readers of *Smash Hits* magazine voted them the worst band in Britain that month.

While there was still talk of a European tour in the summer of 2000, it seemed apparent that the UK concerts were their last. Victoria was so overcome with sadness that after their last concert at London's Earls Court she shed tears on stage, thinking no doubt of good times past and good times gone. Even more distressing was news of the death of a rigger who fell as he was dismantling the band's stage set after their last concert at Earls Court. The accident seemed a tragic epitaph for the death of the band. So when the girls unveiled statues of themselves in the Rock Café they were just going through the motions – professional smiles, private distance.

While the girls have an album out in autumn 2000 and a double A-side Christmas single, there is a sense that they keep going for the sake of appearances. However the money doesn't seem to stop rolling in for any of them. Victoria can rely on an income from a string of companies in addition to Spice Girls Limited, including Spice Girls Productions, Spice Girls Merchandising, Spice Girls Perfumes, Spice Girls Touring and Octopus Direct. She has also set up the ironically named Moody Productions through which to pursue her solo interests.

All five girls were planning their independent ventures and Victoria had a bit of catching up to do in pursuit of her solo career. Unsure of her singing ability, it was not at first certain that she would follow in the same path as the four other girls and go solo. She tried television and film before going back to her singing roots. While she turned down the chance to appear as a stand-in presenter for *The Big Breakfast* TV show, she did spend several weeks filming for her own TV documentary programme, *Victoria's Secrets*. Even so she has kept one eye on the film world, auditioning for numerous parts, including remakes of *Charlie's Angels* and *What's New Pussycat?*, and reading a number of scripts. She emphasized that far from being typecast in a glamorous role she would much prefer to try her abilities as a comedian, playing a 'wacky, dippy' role in a movie.

The only kind of parts on offer involved appearing nude or taking part in a love scene, which her husband would never allow. As she says: 'I think he would find that very hard.' It seemed Victoria's film career was getting nowhere, and although *Victoria's Secrets* had garnered reasonable reviews it was more of a curiosity than a career move.

She had meetings with various media movers and shakers in London and Los Angeles, including Hollywood director Oliver Stone, and has taken the time to have acting lessons with a coach in Primrose Hill, North London. 'They're a lot of fun,' she said. 'I'm taking my time on what to do outside the Spice Girls as I don't want to make any mistakes.'

Victoria was finding out the hard way that success as a pop singer may open doors but does not guarantee success as an actress. Gamely, she has come back from numerous disappointments. When she went to audition for the part of Lara Croft, the cyber girl, she was really excited about the possibility of spending months filming in exotic locations. As part of the role, she would have had to have lessons in martial arts so that she would be able to do the complex fighting moves herself. So she must have been bitterly disappointed not to get the part.

In a way she has Sir Alex Ferguson to thank for kick-starting her solo singing career. After his bust-up with David, Victoria realized that, whatever she may want, she had to spend more time in the north for the sake of her husband's career. In order to make the best of a bad job, it was suggested that she link up with singer Gary Barlow who lived nearby in Cuddington, Cheshire. At first she was extremely reluctant. The former Take That singer has had a terrible roasting in the media over the last couple of years, his singing stardom eclipsed by former colleague Robbie Williams. Victoria may have been afraid that if the meetings were publicized they would be presented as a desperate attempt to shore up a failing career. But in fact their song-writing union worked well, Victoria recording several ballads with him. It inspired her to travel to Los Angeles to work with songwriter Rhett Lawrence for her first solo album. A new career beckons for Mrs Beckham.

It's 2 a.m. on Sunday morning in London's West End at the Astoria Theatre, Charing Cross Road. Posh Spice is about to launch her new single, 'Out Of Your Mind'.

Outside, it's a hot and humid August night, the streets are still teeming with people.

Inside it's G.A.Y. club night at the Astoria. The sweaty dance floor and the stage are packed with 1,500 people, mostly boys, dancing together, face to face, front to back, kissing, stroking, grinding. The temperature rises when the exhibitionist element in the crowd who are dancing on stage are given their marching orders to make way for the queen of the night, Posh Spice. The expectation is palpable; there is a film projection on the back wall of the stage, showing clips from *Victoria's Secrets*. You can't hear it over the thumping dance music. The tension builds and a dance mix of Geri's hit, 'Bag It Up' comes on. One wonders whether Victoria had sanctioned that choice. The audience loves it. The boys have always loved the Spice Girls, since the heady days when they launched their career under the auspices of G.A.Y. club night, singing 'Wannabe', the single that made their name and their millions. As club promoter Jeremy Joseph, who also organized Emma's first solo gig, says: 'There's a lot of nostalgia for them.'

The strains of Geri fade out and Dane Bowers performs an energetic version of his recent hit 'Buggin'. Then the lights go down and the smoke machines are pumped up as black dancers wearing miners' helmets surround a very slim, gold-clad figure centre stage. It is Posh. She performs, or rather mimes, her single and she and the dancers go through a very tight, obviously well-rehearsed dance routine including funky, well-manicured hand movements. The crowd cheers, they want more. And they get it. David Beckham is beamed up on the screen behind the stage saying some kind words about his wife, which are drowned out by the noise of the enthusiastic crowd. The boys know who they really really want.

She nearly drives them wild when she cries out, 'Do you think David's an animal in bed?' To ear-splitting whistles being blown by most of the crowd Victoria graciously comes back on stage for an action replay of her new song. She goes through the same motions all over again. Clearly not a huge repertoire yet.

Round the back at the stage door there was a small but well-behaved scrum of gay boys and a few teenage girls, who had obviously been loyal Spice Girls fans since the good old days. They crowded round the door hoping for autographs. The press photographers hovered, then ran off to the tabloid picture desks. Victoria's less than polite entourage of minders and drivers played the part of thugs or henchmen, aggressively ordering the small crowd to stand aside for her silver Mercedes limousine. There was a lot of foul and aggressive language, hardly suitable for such young ears. She smiled and signed a few posters for her handful of fans and was swept away down the alley into the night.

Victoria's frantic endeavours to ensure that her first solo single hit number one said much about her life and her character. With the gradual decline of the Spice Girls, she had perhaps the most difficult journey of all the group. As the other girls brought out solo singles and albums, Victoria had stayed in the musical background. It would have been all too easy to slip into the shadow of her husband, to become a famous mother who used to sing and dance. There would have been no disgrace in that route.

But that would be to underestimate her drive and energy. Although she is no more ambitious than the others she is perhaps without Mel C's natural talent or Geri's individualism. Victoria showed a lot of guts to take the plunge and go it alone. 'I'm not the best singer or the best dancer in the world, but I work hard,' she says.

At the same time she is a woman who likes to have a group around to support her, be it her family, her husband or the other Spice Girls. Indeed at times her body language on TV or her language in radio interviews betrays that innate nervousness at being the centre of attention. Conversely attention is what she craves and attention is what she gets. Everyone and everything was exploited in her drive to succeed. Her husband was revealed as a gay icon, her son was conveniently photographed on a day out at the zoo days before the song was released. Then there was her claim that her husband sang on the record, the 'did he, didn't he?' saga occupying hundreds of column inches. Which was precisely the object of the exercise. Just as she said that David would streak naked around Old Trafford if the single hit number one.

It didn't stop there. When her single was released in August it was hard to avoid Victoria Beckham as she careered around the country on a promotional tour like a woman possessed. In a week she travelled an estimated 8,000 miles, signing her single in stores around the country as well as flying to Ibiza for a gig. When she and David appeared at Woolworths in Oldham to promote her efforts, the *Sun* newspaper described her in a banner headline as 'Desperate'. There was glee too when it was revealed that her friend, *OK!* magazine owner Richard Desmond, had given his staff cash to buy copies of the single in various stores, and further amusement when a mystery woman bought thirty-four copies of the single at a Woolworths branch near Victoria's home. While her mother denied accusations that she had attempted to rig the charts, the impression was left that Victoria would do anything, say anything to win the battle for number one. In spite of her efforts she failed by a whisker, her rival Spiller taking the number one slot, Victoria having to make do with silver. 'It's made us feel great that Posh Spice felt so threatened that she had to pull out so many tricks to get publicity,' said her Spiller rival, Sophie Ellis-Bextor, who added insult to injury by wearing a T-shirt that read 'Peckham'.

Victoria may have lost the battle but she seemed to have won the war inside herself, for the first time proving that she could perform on her own, could attract the crowds on her own merits. In Oldham for example police horses were called in to control the estimated 6,000 fans who had gathered to see her and her husband. As she admitted: 'Usually if I'm with the Spice Girls, I think all the crowds are there to see Emma or Melanie, but for the first time people are there to see me and it's really flattering.'

She was emerging from the long shadows of self-doubt and the collective safety of the Spice Girls. At the same time her need to control everything about her life may be one reason why the Beckhams launched legal proceedings against my publisher and me. Her inborn insecurity, be it in her marriage or her career, contributed to the manic round of self-promotion. Driven by ambition, fuelled by insecurity, Victoria Beckham is a formidable young woman, but when the doubts crowd in, her husband is always there as a foil and comfort.

Separately they were stars, together they are a luminous couple who light up the social landscape. At times she may be hell to live with but they are a match made in tabloid heaven.

Index

INDEX